# The Tokens of Esteem

# The Tokens of Esteem

An Essay in Ritual Inhumanity

*Patrick D. Harvey*

Writers Club Press
San Jose New York Lincoln Shanghai

# The Tokens of Esteem
## An Essay in Ritual Inhumanity

Writers Club Press
an imprint of iUniverse, Inc.

For information address:
iUniverse, Inc.
5220 S. 16th St., Suite 200
Lincoln, NE 68512
www.iuniverse.com

I have quoted two authors directly in this essay. The great nobel laureate Octavio Paz in his magnificent work El Laberinto de la Soledad and the great French writer Pierre Vidal-Naquet in his incisive treatment of the holocaust controversy, Les Assassains de la Memoire. Translations of these brief passages may be found in the "notes" at the end.

ISBN: 0-595-22288-9

Printed in the United States of America

*This book is dedicated to the memory of my paternal grand-father, Joseph Herman Harvey*

Omnis enim, qui mala agit, odit lucem et non venit
ad lucem, ut non arguantur opera eius.

Secundum Ioannem

3:20

Novem Testamentum Latine

"All, then, who do evil, hate the light and do not
come toward the light, that their deeds may not be
made known"

John

3:20

Latin New Testament

# Contents

# Foreword

This essay is not intended to be a scholarly work although it does draw upon the works of numerous scholars in the fields of anthropology, history and behavioral science. Rather it is intended as a popular analysis of a phenomenon that has occurred since the dawn of time, namely the use of inhumanity in human religion and magic. Many of the practices of our primitive forbears have been viewed with great horror and disgust as barbaric and inhumane atrocities.

Although these events and practices have had their parallels in the modern world we have always considered them to be unacceptable. Such rites as head hunting, cannibalism, human sacrifice and the use of human organs as ornaments, have no place in modern society except among the most twisted and perverse characters. In ancient and prehistoric times, however, they were accepted as quite ordinary and beneficial to society and to mankind in general.

Their practice had something of a holistic and integrating effect upon ancient peoples. The ritual, however inhumane, brought the members of the tribe or clan together, gave them a collection of ceremonies with which to define the operation of their cultures and helped them to deal with the nature of impermanence in the world about them. The rites among primitives were a simple mechanism to make sense out of a world that was much harsher and unforgiving that that of our own.

We all have our rituals. They exist in our houses of worship, work, and leisure and in our private lives. Without ritual we could not long survive as a culture. This was equally true for primitive peoples many of whom found a certain comfort in these practices. This was a comfort that allowed them to continue and to develop their lives and civilizations

# *Preface*

In these modern days there are many who define the concept of self-esteem, rather loosely, as a kind of glad-hand, feel-good, me-me-me self-expression. Even some professionals favor the yuppie-boomer ego trip as a satisfactory lifestyle goal. In this essay, however, self-esteem is portrayed with a little less glamour.

Among the primitives and ancients esteem was focused upon two factors, the individual and his relationship to the group. The renowned psychoanalyst, Karl Menninger, once described mental health as a high level of personality integration. There are many different facets to personality. They include physical, emotional and spiritual features as well as a plethora of factors affected by external causes. Self-esteem is that recognition of personal merit and control that allows the individual to successfully blend these factors in a framework that he can use to cope, in a practical way, with the world. He can respond effectively to its challenges and assault. On the group level self-esteem becomes important because it is the device by which an individual becomes a viable member of the group and a contributing partner in the society in which he has been reared.

Dr. Menninger wrote that a serial, psychotic killer kills, not because he is crazy, but to keep from going crazy. That is to say that the act of killing is the method he uses to reintegrate his personality so that his personality does not entirely disintegrate. In much the same manner the primitive peoples of the earth used ritual killing and other types of inhumanity to integrate themselves. The difference is that their effort was a communal one and a function of integration rather than an isolated one that resulted from alienation.

The primitive and the psychotic are similar but they are not the same. The primitive was on the path to civilization whereas the psychotic had been abandoned by civilization and, in turn, had abandoned the codes of moral and ethical behavior that might have curtailed his bloodthirsty impulses. It is a small distinction, perhaps, but an important one. Eventually the primitive cultures advanced and abandoned their blood lust for more peaceful solutions to their anxieties. The psychotic can not do the same.

Ritual inhumanity was one of the ways in which primitives achieved the level of self-esteem necessary to integrate their own personalities and then integrate themselves into the group. This essay is about some of the practices that they employed to achieve those ends.

# *Acknowledgements*

I should like to thank all of those very fine history professors who taught me when I was young. They are the ones who inspired this book. Also I give acknowledgements to the public library systems of Muscogee County in Georgia and Mecklenberg County in North Carolina. It was their resources and reference computers that made this work possible. Lastly I should thank my sisters, Catherine, Ann and Ellen whose computers I used, over the years, to compose and edit this work.

# Introduction

There is a need for ritual. Man becomes a person by establishing, through his participation in ritual, a relationship with the rest of his kind. Despite the changes which have ensued during the countless millennia in which man has been on this planet the need remains. The psychologists say that the individual needs to belong. No individual would function optimally without the presence of others of his species. It is this sense of belonging that reinforces the need for ritual, the need for some mechanism whereby the continuity of existence can be sustained. The individual must have some assurance that he will find meaning and substance in his life. In the course of human social development it has always been ritual that has provided this assurance. The need for ritual is obviously reflected in the growth of modern industrial states. There exists a separation of individuals into ideological camps. The existence of these separate ideological components very often hinders good cultural health. In some countries these factions are capable, in a single political move, of completely changing the form of government. In other communities factionalism tends to suppress certain groups such that they experience intense social distress. The holistic communal experience is so diminished that people have killed one another wantonly just to reinforce their own beliefs.

Among modern men, there have been instances of inhumanity that far outweigh any barbarism committed by their primitive antecedents in the name of communal solidarity. These aptly demonstrate the consequences of ideological factionalism in the modern world. How many civil wars in how many different lands, where father killed son and brother butchered brother, were brought into being in the name of Ideology?

Ideologies have value and place in the modern world. In fact, ideology is important to social progress because it is, and always has been, a precipitator of change. In the cultural development of human beings change is the most critical factor. But change, which often comes fast and furious, is not always socially healthy. The value of tradition and ritual, even in these sophisticated times, is in its ability to moderate viewpoints and the changes which opinion and belief engender.

A final peril with which modern societies are faced is the danger of alienation. In a primitive, integrated society it was not usually possible for an individual to be outside his group socially and still survive. People relied too heavily upon one another for their very survival. In a society in which the initial phases of ideological development are beginning to appear, dissatisfaction is usually resolved by attachment to a specific group which, by its policy, defines or redefines the individual's social role. Very often the success of an ideological movement depends upon its ability to satisfy the social needs of its adherents. In that case alienation is discarded in favor of a new social role.

The danger here is that the person is not likely to consider the ethical value of his participation because his need for acceptance has overshadowed his sense of judgment. This is the case with many obviously good people who joined the Nazi Party or the Ku Klux Klan. In a society in which the cultural development has extended beyond ideological factions, such as in our own post-industrial society, the individual is forgotten in a maze of technological litter. We must all strive to recognize the right and the need of the individual to strive for identity and expression. His personal identity and its legitimate expressions are the truest forms of the *Tokens of Esteem.*

# 1

# *Choices*

Among the many enemies of the Ancient Roman Empire were a group of nomadic warriors called Celts, or Gauls. Anyone familiar with Caesar's <u>Gallic Wars</u> will recall the Celts. These ancient denizens of the primeval forest were a fierce and bloodthirsty people, both gruesome and enterprising in their pursuits. Consider the arts of war and head hunting. Warriors proved their prowess in battle by decapitating their slain opponents. Such trophies were worn on the belt as ornaments. Skulls were hollowed out, lined with leather or gold and used as drinking cups. Some heads were placed upon poles above the chimneys of Celtic houses to ward off evil spirits. Prisoners of war were killed, mutilated and offered up on sacrificial fires to Celtic gods. Enemy blood was mixed with wine in giant cauldrons and ritually drunk by Celtic warriors. This honor was reserved for those stalwarts who had taken a head in battle.

Thousands of miles and centuries of time distant from the dark and fearsome hollows of the European forests lived another warrior cult, the dark-skinned Manus of Melanesia. The Manus, not quite as fierce or as bloodthirsty as their Celtic cousins, practiced a different style of skullduggery. Their skull cult honored the heads of households rather than defunct adversaries. When a father died, his body was transported to a special site of entombment and there allowed to decompose. The mourners, fearful of the cadaver's evil mana, assiduously avoided all contact with the remains of the deceased. Taboo and ritual purification was strictly observed until the flesh of the father had decayed and only the bone remained. The skull was then removed, hollowed out and placed in a position of prominence in the household. This fetish, representing the spirit of the dead patriarch, was held to protect its mortal charges from harm. Effusive propitiation and proper ceremony guaranteed victory in warfare, fertility in the fields and immunity from disease. The father's anger, caused by the impiety of a recalcitrant mourner, explained every catastrophe. When the son, or living father, died, the old skull was unceremoniously thrown out. Manu belief dictated that the spiritual impotency of the old skull confirmed that the skull was devoid of practical power. Its demonstrated inability to protect the life of its own heir rendered the skull useless.

In the heart of the Amazon, midst the piercing cries of exotic birds and the furtive slithering of bizarre reptiles, there lived a third warrior cult, the Witoto. More bloodthirsty than the Celts and less prayerful than the Manus, the Witoto lived in a constant state of war. Captives were always killed. Their bodies were flayed. The flesh of the arms, legs and trunks was distributed among the warriors. Each combatant received his share on the end of a pointed stick. These trophies were cooked in a boiling pot and then eaten. Only the warriors could partake of this ghoulish cuisine. This anthropophagous digestion was justified with a certain homeopathic rationale. The ritual ingestion of an enemy, however dyspeptic, was believed to imbue the victor with the strength, power and cunning of the vanquished. What virtues he possessed were preserved in the person of his conquerors. In addition, the dismemberment and consumption of an enemy was a demoralizing and humiliating insult to his clansmen. To add further insult the Witoto fashioned necklaces from the teeth of their victims. They stirred cooking pots with their bones.

A divine king ruled a fourth group of warriors. They controlled more geographic space and had a more complex social organization. The Zulu chief wielded absolute power of life and death over his subjects. This accouterment of his imperial office extended even beyond his own lifetime. In death, the monarch was interred with human grave goods. His funeral pyre was a burning pit into which he was cast along with those of his servants who had attended him in life. Nobles of great merit were given the honor of following their master into his slumber. When the mother or the wife of a great Zulu chief died, she was buried with young girls. These young women were still alive during the burial ceremony. In some cases, a living king, who had lost his virile powers, would commit himself voluntarily to the flaming pit. His subjects then benefited from the rule of a younger more potent king.

These examples would not be complete without a brief contribution from Meso-America. The Aztecs also were a noted and worthy warrior cult. From among their war captives, the Aztec priests would select a youth that was remarkable for both his bravery and his physical perfection. This selection was made at the beginning of the Aztec ceremonial year. From the moment of his attachment to the ceremonial rite the young man was accorded every honor and courtesy which the tribal members could think to bestow. He was arrayed in only the finest clothing. Every whim and fancy was granted. Warriors showed him great respect. The people made obeisance toward him as he passed. The Aztec king bowed before the captive. For the Aztecs this chosen one was considered to be the incarnation of the god Tazacatilopca. In honoring the captive the tribe was honoring the god. Toward the end of the year of ceremony, the youth was married to four maidens, each of whom was expected to gratify his every desire. Stated simply, the young man was spoiled rotten.

On the last day of the year the young man was led out of the city to a small temple some distance away. Accompanying him were several priests and warriors. Ascending the pyramid of the temple, he arrived at his intended destiny. Once at the summit of the temple, he was stretched across an altar stone. His chest was incised with an obsidian knife. One priest reached into his rib cage and pulled out his beating heart. This heart was then offered to the god of the temple. The priest next smeared the blood of the victim on the idol of the god. After severing the captive's head, the priest threw the lifeless body down the steps of the temple. Meanwhile, in the city, a new captive was selected to act as a surrogate god for the new ceremonial year.

Far to the north of these blood sacrifices, in what is now the Western Plains area of the United States, the Crow Indians lived their lives in dreams. The Crow religion focused on dream and vision interpretation. Now dreams are quite ordinary and predictable events but visions are very often at a premium. To induce these visions the Crow warrior used continence, self-torture and self-mutilation. Abstinence from food, water, sex and any material comfort was accompanied by isolation in a barren and dismal solitude. In the pursuit of vision the successful candidate gashed pieces of flesh from his body, perhaps even chopping off one or more joints of his fingers. The purpose of the seeker was to discover, through visions, what was to be his function in life and in the tribe. He desired to secure the path that he should follow. The rigor of the pursuit was to insure the truthful interpretation of the dream-state.

These six examples graphically illustrate the practice of ritual inhumanity. Human sacrifice, the use of human parts as ornaments, head hunting, self-mutilation and ritual cannibalism are all shocking, brutal and malapropos. Yet each practice represents part of an integrated culture, a culture which is a synergistic expression of a people and its history. Stanley Diamond, a noted anthropologist, suggested that primitive rituals that favor the killing or mutilation of human beings represent to the participants a personal and a collective experience. This ritual behavior acts as a cathartic and, therefore, a safeguard against the onslaught of social and personal anxiety. These rites are very personal and extend to the victim a very personal sense of humanity, a very intimate involvement in his fate and in his condition. In addition they help to integrate the group more fully because they are never abstract or without feeling or social purpose.

In addition to dealing with the problem of integration, these practices attempted to deal with the phenomenon of impermanence. From season to season and from year to year nature is in a constant state of change. Things come into being and cease to be. As Heraclitus once stated, no man can put his foot in the same stream twice. Where man has perceived himself to be an integral part of the cycles of nature, of birth, death and rebirth, he has surmised that a ritual participation in the cycle might assure his own continuity. The Near Eastern affinity with the Great Mother was, in part, an explanation for human sacrifice. To be a part of death as a ritual affirmation of life and permanence is to be a part of life. The Celts had no fear of death because they believed that the spirits of their dead would be born again as children.

A third factor with which these atrocities deal is the process of cultural selection by exclusion. The specific cultural activities of a group are determined largely by exclusive selection. While there may be a panoply of potential cultural responses to any particular ecological setting, there needs to be a limit on their number and kind. Limitation facilitates both the transaction and the transmission of cultural values. Just as a phonetic alphabet must be limited in sounds to facilitate intelligible expression, so must a culture be limited in its characteristics for its members to deal with one another effectively.

The integration of the individual, the confrontation with impermanence and the selection of cultural activities rely upon choice. This essay is about individuals and groups and some of their choices. Specifically it is about the relationship between shame and self-esteem, between the assertiveness of power and the trembling of fear, between choice and the opportunities for expressing or discharging emotions. The choices to be examined are those which relate directly to the terminal use of part or all of the human body to enhance the esteem of a person, a group or, ceremonially, a god. That is, to use human bodies, in part or all, alive or dead, as the *Tokens Of Esteem*. This consideration is predicated upon the notion that the use of such tokens represents a normative pattern of behavior and cultural development. Such practices pass historically between the advent of Neanderthal Man and the presence of Homo Sapiens. Human sacrifice and human ornamentation are expected developments and are, in some ways, predictable.

This book intends to cover the rather broad range of ritual inhumanity.

Consider integration. In any isolated cultural context the relationship between the individual and his group is most important. The group provides an opportunity for involvement. Involvement does not always insure a satisfactory social experience, nor does it necessarily fulfill personal goals. It does provide a meaningful referent by which one can establish his relationship to the world. One is provided a name, a place and a function. He becomes an individual by examining himself within the context of a social whole. Therein he establishes those references to the group that allow him to perceive himself as an individual. He becomes a person through his comparison with others. That is not to say that his differences with the group make him an individual. Rather he can establish a sense of identity by participation with others. Where the choices are simple the individual ordinarily opts for involvement, This reinforces the proclivities of the group and secures his own position.

If the individual is a function of his culture then he is also an expression of its teachings. The exercise of his cultural prerogatives gives him the greatest satisfaction and is an important element in determining the emotional degree of his societal involvement. Is his relationship to the community a personal one or is it a complementary participation that allows a reasonably autonomous person to act within a collective whole? Does the participant experience a sense of community in whose intimacy integration is favored at the expense of alienation or does he respond diffidently to society that delineates personable relationships into a formalized and ritual experience? In the words of the great Nobel laureate, Octavio Paz, in his El Laberinto de la Soledad:

La repetición de actitudes y fórmulas seculares no solamente asegura la permanencia del grupo en el tiempo, sino su unidad y cohesión. Los ritos y la presencia constante de los espiritus de los muertes entretejen un centro, un nudo de relaciónes que limitan la acción individual y protegan al hombre de la soledad y al grupo de la dispersión. (p.239)

Differences in these two, community and society, can determine the popularity and frequency of ritual inhumanity. The point is this. Very small, communal groups generated ritual inhumanity more fully and frequently than did larger groups. The reason may have been a lack of complexity but the overriding factor was the holistic action of the group. The Jivaro warriors of Ecuador acted as a military unit while head hunting. The preparation of the skull involved boiling the flesh in order to reduce it to perhaps a third of its original size. The resulting shrunken head was returned to the village where it was displayed to the crops and domestic animals. This rite functioned as an increase ceremony. Women, who tended to the domestic concerns, were directly involved. The psychological life of the community was thus sustained. The Jivaro were a very small group. Larger more complex units developed different approaches to ritual.

More complex social units have, numerically, more diversions with which to build and sustain a community profile. Certain levels of social and technological sophistication preclude direct participation in communal concerns in these larger social entities. Priests usually perform the ritual functions as most of the common citizens are engaged in other, more mundane pursuits. Such divisions of labor prevailed among the ancient Incas. Agriculture, manufacturing and trade occupied the interests of the average man. Ritual offerings were limited to priests on specific occasions. For the election of a new emperor two hundred children were sacrificed. In usual times such practices did not occur. Eventually, intensifying patterns of cultural complexity and technological integration engendered social stratification that created specialized ritual. The ceremonial role was relinquished to designated practitioners. Thus groups who take heads exclusively are smaller than those who only take heads in war who are, in turn, smaller than those who take heads punitively. Each progression requires further specialization.

The most widely observed specialist was the shaman, or medicine man. Shamans were tribal members who might be considered as having a certain psychotic disposition. Religion and medicine were in the realm of the shaman. Hence the name witch doctor. The ability to exorcise evil spirits, commune with the dead and journey to the nether world were all skills attributed to the medicine man. These made him the focus of religious and secular life at the communal level. Often he was described as being a good shaman or an evil sorcerer. Many were held in great dread. Sometimes the shaman, accused of practicing black magic, was done in by the tribe. As a focal point the shaman was an important integrative functionary although he, himself, was often detached physically from the tribe. His comings and goings between different worlds were an exception to the identity quest of the individual.

The shaman and his meandering into the spirit world present the problem of impermanence, the reality of change and rebirth. What is the solution to impermanence? Some mythologies suggest the practice of substitution whereby one person is freed from death or pain by inflicting pain or death on another. The exigencies of the divine might therefore be satisfied on an impersonal or other personal basis. Expurgation of sin or disease, a manifestation of sin, from an adult Inca frequently necessitated the sacrifice of his child. Stress filled circumstances required the ancient Phoenicians to offer the children of their great nobles to the fires of Melquart. Even Abraham was asked to offer his son Isaac to Yahweh. Cultural preferences for vicarious compensation makes human sacrifice an important adjunct of the philosophy, take him not me.

The existence of physical impermanence creates a speculative posture toward death. The defunct possessed a spiritual currency among primitive cultures. Body parts of the deceased might be traded, if only through ceremony, for some material or spiritual benefit. The cephalic trophies of Celtic warfare were displayed above the door so the spirit of the defunct enemy might guard the Celtic family. Why should the persona of the slain foe be so indulgent that he would willingly safeguard the prosperity of the warrior who had killed him? An exchange had taken place as a consequence of the prescribed rite. The Celt had preserved, physically, the memory of his adversary. Extolling the virtues of his foe to other warriors, he related how superior a combatant the enemy had been, how powerful, how cunning. Naturally, he does not neglect his own importance. In exchange for the preservation of his memory the victim provided spiritual protection, a kind of supernatural-natural symbiosis between the living and the dead, not dissimilar to ancestor worship.

Many examples of this speculative attitude exist. The preservation of skulls, the use of human bones as amulets, the ritual consumption of human flesh and the immense numbers and ways of burial all point to this exchange with the other world. There is, of course, the obverse side of the coin where speculative exchange is designed, not for the benefit but for the defilement of the deceased. In his life of Solon, the historian and social commentator Plutarch, recounts an illustration. One, Megacles, and his party had committed an injustice against another group called the Cylons. The two parties became embroiled in a conflict in which the side of Megacles received the worst half. Within their assembly the Athenians judged the matter and decided in favor of the Cylons. Those followers of Megacles, who were still alive, were required to pay damages to their opponents, a seemingly just and propitious arrangement. But what of those who had died in the fracas and were already buried? From these defunct the Athenians exacted a different fine. According to Plutarch their bodies were disinterred, carried to the borders of the Athenian Hegemony and, without ceremony, dumped into barbarian territory.

Cultural selection is our third consideration. Unlike integration, selection may be determined by factors not controlled by the group. Hunting communities rely upon the prevalence of game. Agricultural peoples need rainfall and fertility. Manufacturing interests concern themselves with the proximity of raw materials. Trading societies are tied to the means of transportation. All are dependent on the weather and other geographic features. Moreover the choice of one particular endeavor over another, or its preponderance, does not exclude a common factor or common need in selection.

No doubt the selection of choices involves man's perception of himself and his surroundings, a perception which, in part, determines his religious inclinations. In choosing the practice of ritual inhumanity he makes religion the pervasive factor. Secular societies limit their practices to a few groups and a few special occasions. The energies expended to propitiate the supernatural rely upon the attachment to the other world. Religion, incidentally, does not have to be an organized institution with a regular hierarchy, such as the religion of ancient Rome. Association with a particular credo is optional. Simple attachment to ideas not founded in reality and related to chthonic or Ouranic powers will do. Magic, in which words are believed to have power over material things, is often a workable substitute.

Selection factors may become distorted across time and distance. Each group has its own sense of history. Sigmund Freud observed in <u>Totem and Taboo</u> that contemporary primitives may also have their ancient period. We must consider what is ancient to us. We must consider what is ancient to them. The religious and social practices of ethnocentric groups may be in a state of decay, a state of transition or a state of equilibrium. Current practice may be so much a distortion of the original that the two are in no way alike. Comparisons between prehistoric man and modern ethnocentric man are likewise suspect.

Cultural attributes, whether wholesome or destructive, can only be examined in the light of selective exclusion. A particular phenomenon can only be seen in the context of its own culture. The Babylonians, for example, worshipped the god Melquart. The ceremony was harmless. The Phoenicians, who borrowed Melquart from Babylon, turned this worship into a holocaust in which innocent children were fed to the fire god. The Hebrews, which were Semitic cousins of the Phoenicians, were appalled by human sacrifice. Witness the tribulations of Abraham when asked to offer up his son, Isaac.

Time is a critical ingredient. In extremely isolated conditions, where there are few technological advances and limited social contact and where circumstances have created a state of equilibrium, these practices may continue, unabated, for centuries. Human sacrifice in India was extant in Neolithic times and only suppressed by the British in the nineteenth century. Spanish conquistadors suppressed the religious activities of the Incas and the Aztecs in the sixteenth century. The rites of human sacrifice and the pagan version of confession especially appalled them. Yet **La Patria**, a South American newspaper, reported an Inca style human sacrifice in the mining districts of the Andes. The date of the report was June 2, 1960.

Behavior is another factor. Universal rules for behavior are precluded by the separate psychological compositions of societies. The presumption of guiding factors is limited to very basic human dispositions. Catherine Berndt advises us that human beings are individuals irrespective of their particular social status or the nature of their community. No two will react in exactly the same way. Thus ecological compositions of human beings, simple or complex, experience a constant state of flux that precludes the accurate employ of categories. It is more useful to consider man as a cognitive and adaptive being than as an anthropological type. The quality of humanity lies as much in the diversity of its characteristics as it does in a proper nomenclature.

There is, in fact, no physiological or intellectual difference between any groups of people, modern or prehistoric, of any great consequence. The differences in cultural activities and accomplishments are due to restrictions in environment and rates of technological development. It is man who makes the adaptation to his situation. It is the contention of this essay that one very important factor is the pursuit of self-esteem, either individually or collectively. Having a sense of oneself and one's values is the universal reward of all human endeavors. The question becomes one of determining the mechanisms where by esteem is gained. The question becomes one of choices.

# 2

# *All the King's Horses, All the King's Men*

## The Scythians

The barbarian Huns of Attila threatened the peace of the Roman Empire in the fifth century AD and the fierce Mongol horsemen of Genghis Khan swept across Asia in the twelfth century. They are well known to history. They were masters of cruelty. They also displayed superb equestrian skill. The agility and speed of the mounted warriors of the Steppe were common knowledge. Yet one of the earliest peoples to develop the use and cult of the horse lived in the eighth century BC. These nomadic wagon people, whose favorite pastimes were war and horses, established a brief hegemony over parts of Southern Russia in the seventh century BC. They were called the Scythians.

As the Scythians were a nomadic people, lacking any written language or permanent towns, their history is very sparse. Accounts of Greek historians register an extensive contact with the Pontic cities. Archeological records suggest the Scythians had some contact with most major civilizations of their time including the Chinese, Greek, Roman and Persian empires. However peripheral, these encounters do establish a pattern of movement that made the Scythians a people to be reckoned with in the ancient world.

Although they had no permanent living quarters, the Scythians erected massive burial chambers for their chiefs. In a manner similar to the Chinese, these steppe people believed in ancestor worship. They spared little expense and ceremony to inter both commoner and king. Burial grounds were sacred to the Scythian warriors. They were accorded a sanctity that was defended to the death of the last man. Herodotus recounts that the Persian king Darius once taunted the Scythians to come out and fight him in a pitched battle. They replied that they had no cities or towns to defend but that they would fight and kill anyone that dared to defile the resting-places of their kings.

It is the burial rite of the kings that involves a fundamental theme of this essay. The only contemporary account describing these rites was written by Herodotus of Halicanarsus. In his fifth century account of the Persian wars he made the following observations.

When a Scythian king died his body was eviscerated. The stomach was split open, the intestines removed and the innards replaced with sweet herbs and unguents. The corpse was then sewn. This mummification process was necessary because burial rites were performed only in the early spring and autumn. The final stage of embalming was a wax covering poured over the body of the king. Commoners were treated with the same process but with less ceremonial fanfare.

Having been given this preliminary mortuary process, the king's body was placed upon a wagon and driven about the countryside. This allowed all of his faithful followers to view his remains. The mourners gashed themselves, cut flesh from their ears and jabbed arrows into their left hand. The Huns, often confused by ancient chroniclers with the Scythians, gashed their cheeks and ears at funerals. Many of the steppe peoples acted in a similar fashion. The Scythian chieftain was buried in a large pit, one side sloped, the opposite side straight. A small tunnel in the wall served as a burial shaft. Wooden beams were installed against the sides for support. A conical roof was place on top to cover the entire pit to give the tomb a tent like appearance. As time and talent allowed, the grave pit was made to resemble the dwelling of the king as it had been in life. It was supposed that, in death, he would continue in his regal status. The inside walls were covered with rugs or felt. Personal possessions of the deceased were also included.

An inner chamber was constructed to house the body of the dead king. Two side chambers were built. One was constructed to house the personal attendants of the king, the other to provide a place for the grooms. A third chamber was constructed to house the body of the queen who was expected to take her place by the side of her husband. Depending upon the rank and status of the deceased as few as twenty and as many as four hundred horses were killed and buried in the pit. These formed a circle around the human graves.

Typically, the funeral of a chief began with a procession. Standard bearers followed the wagon that bore the king's body. After the standard bearers the tribesman came making loud noises, rattling bells and shields. This was done to frighten away evil spirits. In the wake of the tribesmen were those servants of the king destined to join him in death. The prescribed funeral services were performed and the body placed in the tomb. Human victims were poisoned or strangled and placed in their respective chambers. It is not known if the participation of these human victims was voluntary. The groom held a place of honor in the Scythian world, since he was responsible for the horses. He may have been willing to die with his master. Servants and attendants have often gone the way of their overlords. Loyal wives sometimes joined their husbands in death, voluntarily. Each was placed in the tomb in such a manner as to reflect his station in life.

When the human graves were filled the horses were brought forward, killed and placed around the pit. These horses were the personal property of the monarch and were buried with him as "furniture." Archeological evidence demonstrates that the horses were not lame or otherwise defective, contrary to what one might have suspected. All were prize animals. After the horses were buried, earth was thrown into the pit and the entire burial place was made into a mound. The Scythians concealed the resting-places of their rulers, the ceremonies being conducted, as much as possible, in secret.

Nearly a year later, according to Herodotus, another ceremony took place. Fifty of the king's retainers were killed by strangulation. Their bodies were eviscerated, stuffed with chaff and sewn. Fifty of the king's horses were killed, split open and stuffed in the same manner. Poles were driven through the horses so that all four feet could be raised above the ground and the horses attached to mountings. Poles were also inserted in each of the fifty warriors. Each warrior was then mounted upon a horse and the ensemble was arranged along the perimeter of the gravesite to act as a guardian army.

The kings and queens were buried with great wealth, their personal possessions being mostly of gold and silver. The bodies of the servants, and those of their masters, were arrayed in the finest garments. Herodotus reported that the Scythians disdained bronze and silver in favor of gold although the archeological record does not support his contention. These lavish burials were typical of the Steppe peoples. Even the horses were fitted with leather trappings that were lined with gold and silver. When the Hun died he was buried in like ceremony, supplied with a rich cache of gold and silver items. The workers who dug his grave were put to the sword to insure secrecy. Genghis Khan, buried in a secret place, reportedly went to the hereafter with forty of his slave girls. The Scythians were but the bearers of a custom that had been born long before them and was continued long after.

## The Yellow River Kings

To the east of the lands once proudly roamed by Scythian horsemen lies the alluvial delta of the Yellow River. Twelve thousand years ago this valley came into the Neolithic world. The agricultural revolution swept across the fertile plateau of northern China, transforming the countryside into a primitive farming community. Many small communities maneuvered for position in the struggle for political and economic dominance over this bountiful earth. The first people to establish this control built their capital city at a site now called Anyang.

These conquerors are known to history by the name of their last capital city, Yin. Their political dynasty is called the Shang.

The Shang people were an agricultural people who managed to build a few large cities. The emperor used this urban area as a seat of power. Ordinary citizens used the city as a trade center. Shang communities were socially and economically stratified. Artisans were kept busy creating the highly prized bronzes, characteristic of artifacts found in Shang tombs. Scribes wrote on oracle bones made from the shoulders of oxen. Tokens were used in commerce in lieu of goods and services. The Yin were a literate people, advanced for their times.

Parallel with many early civilizations the Yin had an established aristocracy, not unlike the feudal system of Europe in the Middle Ages. The Yin hierarchy had two great occupations, war and religion. Religion included sacrifice to the gods and ancestors. Ancestor worship was particularly important. Antecedents had the power to cause harm or good. All depended on the treatment they received from their progeny. The oracle bones were used to divine this ancestral will. The purpose of warfare was twofold. First, the Shang believed in the unity of all of China. This meant the subjugation of their neighbors. Second, their religious practices required human victims for sacrifice. The sacrifice of war captives mollified those irate ancestors. Occasionally they were used to strengthen the foundations of buildings. Such unfortunates were used as "cornerstones." Commoners, in the absence of war captives, were used in this fashion.

The Shang people were divided into two classes, the aristocracy and the peasantry. The emperor was the pinnacle of the feudal hierarchy, viewed as the Son of Heaven. The gulf between the commonality and the nobility was immense and impassable. Deference and obedience to authority were mandatory upon pain of death. This class division made the Shang commoner a likely token of esteem. More than one found his way into the burial vault of the nobility.

The burial of king and aristocrat during the Yin period was quite elaborate. In the Anyang district eleven tombs of royalty have been unearthed. The tombs were very large, perimeters measuring fifty by sixty feet. Construction was laid out on a north-south axis, the first pit being dug to a depth of fifteen feet. A second pit, inside the first, was dug to the same depth. The final pit went another eight feet into the earth. Inside this third pit was constructed the wooden burial chamber of the king. The noble warrior was interred surrounded by the accouterments of his high station. Jade carvings and bronze artifacts lay next to the skeletons of horses and dogs.

The horses and dogs are not surprising. The Shang relied heavily upon military power to enforce their will and they were naturally drawn to the hunt. Hunting was the sport of royalty providing excellent training for war. For the nobility hunting was an occupation and an important religious obligation. Li Chi, in <u>The Beginnings of Chinese Civilization</u>, maintained that the remains of male adult humans and dogs were invariably placed underneath the royal burial chamber. This is a fact confirmed by archeology. The royal seal of approval was given to the hunt in Shang society.

In the excavations of these tombs the skeletons of warriors and workers were discovered, along with the usual oriental opulence. The pit directly above the burial chamber contained the bones of humans mixed in with those of animals. The human remains were probably those of the king's servants. Over two thousand such bodies have been unearthed in the royal tombs. From the position of the dead some excavators surmised that the servants were buried alive. Others were decapitated, their skulls placed away from their bodies. These may have been war captives. The style of these burials was connected to the Shang belief in an afterlife. Human and animal grave goods, artifacts and ordinary furniture were needed by the master to carry on his life in the nether world. He would continue to make war upon his enemies. Horses and chariots, attendants and servants, slaves and members of the artisan class would be needed to perform their usual tasks. Warriors to fight for the king would be indispensable.

In the Shang dynasty the funeral service was held with great pomp and circumstance but also in great secrecy. Grave robbers were as expert in China as they were in Mesopotamia and Egypt, despite the plethora of curses and injunctions that may have been invoked on the part of the funeral director. The tomb was covered with piles of earth. This made the burial site appear more like a natural hill, a method employed by the Scythians as well. In the Thirteenth century BC, the Chin overcame the Shang dynasty. The new emperor of the new dynasty continued in the tradition of his ancestors by constructing a lavish tomb for himself and his retinue. All of the workers who built the tomb were buried with their master.

The use of human grave goods in the burial rites of monarchs, such as those of the Scythians and the Shang, is a practice called suttee. The term literally means "true woman." The peoples of India practiced this rite as late as the nineteenth century before the British suppressed it. A true woman demonstrated her loyalty to her deceased husband by throwing herself upon his funeral pyre. She could also jump into his burial pit as it was being filled, thereby expressing her marital fidelity. Although the word suttee generally refers to this Indian rite of self-immolation, in this essay it shall be used to encompass a wider genre of such practices. These include any burial rite in which humans, voluntarily or not, were buried alive with a king, husband, queen, warrior or other person of presumed prominence.

The practice of suttee was ordinarily limited to the burial of persons of great power and authority; nobles that were held in greet esteem. Usually only the king was buried with such rites. Suttee, however, was not limited to any particular cultural or geographic area. The kings of West Africa, the princes of the Incas and the pre-pyramid Egyptian lords were all interred with this practice. Sometimes the practice was performed for the queen or other person in the royal household. In some cultures all warriors of merit were permitted the honor. Commoners were excluded from the ritual honor although they were very often the victims of such rites. That suttee was a function of power can not be denied. In China, the emperor used the ritual killing of commoners to rid his realm of criminals and unruly subjects. He who would defy the emperor would become one of the building blocks of his tomb. In a society such as that of the Scythians participation might have been voluntary. In a society such as China of the Shang the volunteer seems most unlikely.

The text will explore this practice as it relates to the integration of the individual into his community. The most important consideration, however, will be that concerning the problem of impermanence. That the rite attempts to deal with the problem of death is indisputable. Cultural selection was also a factor although the practice was very limited in historical times. As civilizations advanced or were Christianized suttee died out. There are other, more elaborate and more ancient examples of this ritual.

The Royal Graves at Ur

The grave goods with which a person was buried indicated his social class or position. A poor man had little more than a coarse blanket to cover his bones. Priceless treasures surrounded a rich noble. The excavations at Ur in Mesopotamia by Sir Charles Leonard Woolley in the 1920's unearthed several thousand graves dating from the fourth millennium BC. Most were of the commoner type. The body was invariably laid in a position of sleep, drinking cup near his mouth. Included might be a dagger or a few household articles. He went to his death as if on a journey. In later times the dead were buried under the floor of the house. Their spirits were thought to dwell with the family. For the times and people these practices demonstrate nothing out of the ordinary.

The principal difference between the burial of commoner and noble was the wealth of grave goods. There might be a finely worked wooden coffin instead of a blanket, golden drinking vessels rather than cups of clay, weapons made of precious metals instead of bronze. The body was laid out in the same position of sleep. The dead noble's personal cylinder seal, a mark of class, was placed in the tomb. Both noble and commoner intended to spend their deaths as they had spent their lives. For the times and the people this was not extraordinary.

Among the thousands of graves at Ur there were sixteen which Woolley described as Royal Graves. Unlike the graves of commoners and nobles, the royal graves, those suitable for the burial of a king, were built of stone. The tomb was set in the middle of a large pit. The limestone blocks of the royal tombs were not found in the surrounding valley area. They had been transported from thirty miles away, at a considerable expense. Even the Ziggurats, which served as temples to the gods, were made of burnt mud brick rather than stone. The king, considered a god, was exalted above all, exalted in death as he had been in life. His station required the use of the precious limestone for his gravesite.

The death of the god king was viewed as a translation of his life into another form of existence. His tomb was therefore furnished with that thought in mind. The tomb was very richly decorated. Everyday articles such as saws, chisels, bowls, cups and tables were made of silver and gold. Bronze sculptures depicting the king and his works were carved on the walls. War chariots, elaborately decorated, were buried with the very horses that pulled them. Spears were tipped with points made of silver and gold. The tomb of A-Bar-Gi, dating from 3200, was filled with treasures that might well rival that of the Egyptian, Tut-Ak-Amun.

Within these elaborate Royal Graves, Woolley found evidence of suttee. In the burial pits of A-Bar-Gi and his queen, Shu-Bad, more than one hundred bodies were discovered. These remains were apparently the faithful servants who had followed master and mistress into the world beyond. The royal vault made no provision for grave goods of any but those of the king and queen. The attendants were the grave goods! This "furniture" of royalty carried nothing with them but their loyalty to the crown. Woolley believed that these people were not commoners but citizens of high rank who had gone of their own volition to the death chamber. Each attendant was placed in the tomb according to his function. The soldiers were lined in neat rows, each wearing armor and weapons. They were strategically placed in the grave pit to act as guards. Ladies in waiting were dressed in fine robes and beautiful ornaments. They were arranged as they might have been in life, each waiting upon the queen. The grooms of the king's horses stood next to the horses. Chariot drivers dutifully manned their stations. Even the king's cupbearer was in his accustomed place waiting to serve his leader with fresh drink.

There was something even more astounding about this spectacle. There were no indications of duress! There must have been a few recalcitrant servants who had no desire to die on that day. The excavators determined that the attendants went into death voluntarily. At least the archeological evidence suggests such compliance. Perhaps they had been induced into a semi-conscious state. Woolley has suggested the use of opium or hashish. The scene was laid out so meticulously, every small item in exactly the proper place, that someone must have come into the tomb after all were dead and put the "final touches" on everything. Each servant had carried a small cup, some of clay, others of gold or silver. A large cauldron had been placed at the bottom of the pit. All the menials may have been given some potion from the cauldron during the funeral services and later went to sleep in their assigned positions. It is not unlikely that the servants may have been rehearsed in this service.

In another grave, designated PG-1237, six soldiers were found at the entrance to the sloped burial pit. Beneath them four female skeletons were arranged around a large copper cauldron. Within the pit sixty-four court ladies were laid in neat rows. Each woman wore a ceremonial headdress, gold earrings, silver hair bands and sleeved coats of scarlet. Apparently each lady of the court had entered the tomb carrying her cup. She was served some lethal elixir by one of the four women standing by the cauldron. Having drunk her portion she joined her sisters at the bottom of the grave pit. Perhaps the soldiers were at the entrance to insure that everything went according to plan.

From his excavations of these graves, Woolley was able to surmise a probable funeral ritual. The body of the King was interred in its limestone tomb. With the monarch went his personal attendants. The door to the tomb was sealed and a ritual service performed. In one instance the investigators found that victims had been killed and laid over the earth upon which the tomb was built. These "cornerstones" were probably placed there long before the king had died. Earth was then thrown in to cover the tomb, although the level of earth was not made level with the top of the grave pit. A building was then constructed over the tomb, partially filled with packed clay, and used for a second ceremony. Offerings were placed on the bare earth of this second level. These included a human who was sacrificed. These offerings were then covered with earth and the earth tamped. On the next level another human was killed as a sacrifice. These remains were covered with earth. Over the entire subterranean structure a chapel was erected where worshipers came to pay homage to the dead king. Each burial stage was marked by a separate religious ceremony. Woolley believed this was the ordinary burial practice for kings. Monarchs only were honored with such ceremonies.

Some scholars have asserted that the burials of A-Bar-Gi and Shu-Bad were part of a fertility rite involving the Tammuz-Innana myth. The implication is that the bodies representing the monarchs were actually substitutes for the king and queen. This practice was not uncommon. Peoples as far apart as the Persians and the Aztecs practiced such rites. To accept the argument is to discount the practice of suttee among the early Sumerians. As the Sumerians were one of the first civilized peoples to engage in this elaborate ritual and since the affair was carried out in such elaborate detail and with such great expense, it seems only appropriate to refute the idea of fertility rites.

In Sumerian literature there is no record of human sacrifice. (The burial of Gilgamesh is an exception. Suttee is implicit rather than defined in this account). The only physical evidence is that in the Royal Graves at Ur. Had this burial been a vicarious sacrifice there would have been more archeological evidence. Religious texts would have prescribed appropriate rituals. There are only sixteen royal graves and no texts. Had the female body been a substitute for the earth goddess she would have been a young virgin. The skeleton of Queen Shu-Bad was forty-five years of age. Had substitution taken place both male and female elements would be present in all of the tombs. There were several tombs in which only one of the royal partners was present. The final argument is decisive. All tombs contain the royal cylinder seal of the king, the symbol of his power. With this tool he affixed his signature to all official documents. The king would not have put this powerful instrument in a grave while he lived nor would he allow a duplicate of the royal seal to be buried. The conclusion from these arguments is that the burials were those of the monarchs they represent, an ancient example of suttee among civilized peoples.

The royal tombs at Ur date from 3500 BC. Toward the end of 3200 BC the graves were no longer used. Commoner graves were sunk into the same mounds that held the royal graves. For five thousand years the royal graves were lost to history. The practice of suttee continued in Mesopotamia. The tombs of Dungi and his son, Bur Sin, dating from 2300 BC, were built with two burial chambers. One chamber held the body of the king. In the other vault a number of bodies were scattered about. Woolley surmised that the bodies were buried at the same time. Later cuneiform texts confirmed this rite. In the manner of their earlier counterparts, the kings of the third dynasty of Ur were deified and so entitled to these honors. By 500 BC the city of Ur was little more than a temple-city where a few priests kept the old faith alive.

Prehistoric Man

When prehistoric man first conceived of an after life is uncertain but his extensive and widespread burial places indicate that he considered the problem seriously. Food offerings, weapons and ornaments found in prehistoric burial sites demonstrate that the prehistoric concept of death was one in which life continued in another world. The use of ocher, a rust colored iron ore, as a substitute for blood, smeared on the bodies of Paleolithic skeletons affirms his belief in this relationship between the here and the hereafter. The use of the skull and the separation of the skull from the trunk, giving rise to skull cults, reflect the same thinking.

As prehistoric man had no complex political or social systems, his practice of suttee was limited to a familial setting. Numerous double and triple graves have been found containing the remains of man and wife. Both were usually buried at the same time. While this is not unusual even in our own day it does imply the possibility that some wives were unwilling or premature partners in the burial. In Germany, at Baundorff, a male skeleton was found buried; the ashes of a female resting close by. These remains were from the megalithic period. The wife was perhaps provided as a companion to the man. The fact that she was cremated while her husband was interred intact may support some kind of sacrifice. The Vikings practiced this kind of ritual as late as the tenth century AD.

Harz mountain investigators found the skeleton of a woman lying next to that of a man. Marks on the woman's skull indicated that her head was struck with a blunt instrument. Near the lake of Geneva stone chests were uncovered which contained the bodies of a man, woman and child. All were buried at the same time. Johannes Maringer, in The Gods of Prehistoric Man, suggested that the woman and child represented some sort of grave goods although it is equally likely that all three died at the same time. Saint Just Pequart found a grave in which the skeleton of a man and a child were interlaced, the child being cradled in the right arm of the man and the child's feet in his right hand. He found a similar grave in which a woman clutched a child's skeleton. The arrangement of adult and child was the same as in the first example. This is, admittedly, scant evidence for suttee. A better argument might simply be infanticide. If the child's parent died, leaving no one to care for the child, the infant may have been killed for economic reasons. Henri Martin found an interesting example in the cave at La Rue de Sers. The skeletons of a man, age 50, a woman, age 40, and a young man, age 18, were all buried together. This age grouping rules out the possibility of infanticide though not accident.

The reader is cautioned to observe that the foregoing instances of communal burial did not all occur in the same place or time. Pre-history is a span of time covering thousands of years. Before the agricultural revolution people lived in very small communities and had minimal contact with neighboring communities. Culture and tradition were limited. All one can say of this period is that the practice of suttee was a likely cultural option. However, there are two examples in which the practice of suttee seems valid. The crowning touch was discovered at Los Murcielagos. In a secluded cave the skeleton of a woman was stretched across the floor. On her skull was a crown of gold. Around her body, in a semi-circle, lay the bodies of twelve other women; each dressed in fine attire, each with a similar headdress. The lady was obviously of royalty and had been followed in death by her court ladies.

In the British Isles, at a burial mound called Belos Knapp, a different kind of burial was found. The mound had been formed into chambers each housing the bodies of a number of people. Their skulls were all of the dolich-cephalic type (long-headed) suggesting that they were of the same racial stock. The mound was a collective burial site. In one of the chambers was the skeleton of a youth. His skull was of the brachy-cephalic (broad-headed) type, suggesting that he was a different race. E.O. James believed that the youth may have been a sacrifice during some funeral rite as he obviously did not belong to the main group

Thus far we have considered the practice of suttee among prehistoric peoples and among those peoples who might be thought of as being highly civilized. (The Egyptians practiced this rite briefly during the pre-pyramid dynasties.) Now we turn our attention to some of those peoples whose civilizations were less civilized. The two chosen for purposes of illustration are the Vikings and the Thracians. These two groups were nomadic, warrior peoples. They relied upon war as their principal economic and social activity. As they were organized into much smaller social groups than were their agricultural neighbors their relationships were much more personal. Hence the practice of suttee among them was also highly personal and selective.

The Vikings

The explanation of suttee among the Vikings relies upon three factors; the acquisition of wealth and property, traditionally rigid class division and the notion of separate afterlife residences based upon social rank. Since Viking literally means pirate, the acquisition of wealth was by force, any commodity of value being a kind of money. Slaves were an important part of Viking society since they represented a mobile currency that could be used to purchase other kinds of wealth. Slaves were also a principal manifestation of wealth. A Viking, wishing to be buried with his wealth, might take a slave or two with him into the afterlife. Excavated ship burials of the Viking Age suggest that the deceased would carry on in the after life as he had in his earthly life. He would function as a warrior. He was buried with his jewelry, weapons, his ship and his horse. Clothing and food were provided for his journey. Viking queens were no exception. At Osberg Ship Mound, constructed in the ninth century AD, the Viking queen Asa was interred. Her burial was conducted in a most imperious manner. The service included the entombment of one of her slaves.

Slaves, like thralls, were at the bottom of the social hierarchy. Women fared poorly at all levels because they were in service to the warrior caste. The tenth century account of an Arab writer, Ibn Rustah, describes the burial of a great chief among the Rus Vikings. This burial included the entombment of his wife. She was still alive when the grave was sealed. Gwn Jones says that many wooden burial chambers, including the bodies of a man and woman, bear out this practice as described by Ibn Rustah.

The Viking warrior believed that when he died he would go to Valhalla. There, he would continue to fight as a warrior during the day. If he were killed he would rise at the end of the day and proceed, with his comrades, to feast at Odin's table. The following day battle would begin anew. Those who died of sickness or age went to Hel, while virgins had a special place of their own. In any event, the Viking needed his wife or some other servant to look after his personal needs at Valhalla. Perhaps the most vivid description of this practice among the Vikings is that of Ibn Faladn, an Arab secretary to the embassy from the Kaliph of Baghdad to the Bulgars. The Bulgars had extensive contact with the Rus, a connection that made Ibn Faladn's observations possible. The account describes the burial of a Rus chief but may just as well have described the burial of any worthy and noble Jarl.

When a Rus Chieftain died his body was buried in a temporary grave. This initial burial lasted for ten days. Ibn Faladn says that the body turned black in the ground but did not decompose. No embalming methods were employed. The extreme cold of the lower Volga River area made the ground function as a freezer year round. (The secondary burial was cremation. The body would not remain intact indefinitely. The Vikings burned their dead because they could not harbor the thought of the body being eaten by worms and insects.) During the first phase the estate of the deceased provided great quantities of an intoxicating beverage for the mourners. A second part of the revenues from the dead chief's property was used to pay for his funeral accouterments. The third was given over to his family for their support. The wife, of course, would join her husband in the grave.

Elaborate preparations were made for the burial of the chief. Special garments were sewn. A ship was prepared to receive the corpse and send him on his way to Valhalla. The vessel was pulled onto the shore, decorated in accordance with the position of the chief. A special pavilion was constructed on board with a couch upon which the body would rest during the final ceremony. Assignments were made to collect the firewood that would be necessary to kindle the ship. Everyone who was connected with the departed warrior had some specific task if only to feast and drink to his swift departure to Odin and Valhalla.

From among the female slaves of the chief one was asked to volunteer as his companion. Once a volunteer was found she was taken aside and placed in the custody of two older women. The commitment was final and could not be reversed. This slave girl was lavishly adorned as would befit the companion of a great Viking chief. She was indulged in every way. With the mourning kinfolk, she gave herself up to drink, feasting and carnal pleasure. Her funeral duties required a visit to each of the pavilions in which the mourners were housed for the occasion. She would have sexual intercourse with the head of each household. This venery was obligatory on the part of the tent masters and the girl, being performed for the benefit of the dead chief. This was possibly a mechanism designed to ceremonially connect the afterlife with the present. The girl was instructed to tell the deceased (after she had gone with him to Valhalla) that his kinsmen had faithfully discharged their duty.

When the ten days had passed the dead man was disinterred, brought to the ship and placed upon his couch. Kinsmen then killed two chickens, a rooster, two cows, two horses and a dog. These were placed on the ship. The slave girl was brought aboard, violated by six of the kinsmen of the chief and then strangled with a cord. The execution itself was done by an old woman called the angel of death. During the ten-day funeral rite she had been one of the older women who had looked after the slave girl and instructed her in the sacred duties. The mourners then brought fire and timber to burn the ship. This cremation allowed the Viking chief to enter Valhalla directly rather than having to wait for the slower effects of decomposition in the ground. The sexual aspects of this ceremony may suggest a similar thought. The deceased was conceived and reborn immediately in the next world. There are in fact many mythologies in which there is a clear relationship between death, rebirth and sex.

Not all Vikings were buried in this manner. Many were buried with their ship, wife and horse in the typical burial mound. Others died in battle where their bodies were not recovered. This contingency was covered by the Norse belief that a warrior who died in battle went directly to Odin. (Similar to the Moslem belief that a warrior of Allah went directly to paradise if he fell in the Jihad.) Nor did the Vikings achieve the massive burial of slaves and others in their tombs. Their political structure was not as complex as other monarchies. Each Jarl was his own man, gaining power and prestige at the expense of his neighbor and having only a loose association with his chief. This association depended upon the ability rather than the birth or wealth of the leader. Secondly, the Vikings were traders in slaves. They did not wantonly destroy a commodity that might turn a handsome profit. Lastly the influence of Christianity ameliorated many of these brutal practices.

## The Thracians

Suttee was not always socially inclusive. Not just any slave or servant was a candidate. Its exclusive nature is illustrated by the practice among the Thracian aristocracy. In the thousand years before Christ, in what is now Bulgaria, the Thracians practiced hero cult worship. The king-priest-hero, usually a tribal patriarch, was venerated as father, leader and god. Dionysus, so popular with the Greeks, was said to be a Thracian hero turned deity. The king-priest was the apotheosis of temporal and spiritual power. Immortality, a subject defined by the king, was the exclusive province of the aristocracy. Membership in a dynastic family, of which there are eighty mentioned by Herodotus, was the only way to heaven. At least this was so for the men.

The king, and his nobles, engaged in hunting and warfare. Thracians plundered wealth from their neighbors. Weapons were a mark of social distinction, horses a symbol of wealth and class. The possession of toreutic jewelry, weapons and bronze reliefs was a guarantee of the king's favor. Anyone could conceivably raise himself to the peerage by the adept demonstration of military prowess. Herodotus reported that the aristocratic families of Thrace changed in number and size with the vicissitudes of fortune. In any event, the right of suttee was a familial and aristocratic indulgence. Although many Thracian burial mounds remain unexplored the practice of suttee has been demonstrated by excavation and is thought to be universal among the Thracians.

Each Thracian noble had several wives. When the noble died the friend of the deceased decided which of his wives had been the most loyal and beloved. The successful candidate was taken to the grave of the bereaved. Over the grave of her husband the man's friends cut her throat. Her body was buried along side that of her husband as a reward for her fidelity and zeal. The remaining wives, not given this honor, were considered disgraced and the noble community regarded them with general ridicule and scorn. Had the Thracians been able to transcend their tribal phase and unite into a kingdom suttee might have evolved into the kind practiced by the Chinese and Scythian kings. They were unable to achieve this development before their culture was radically affected by outside influences. The Thracians were subdued by the Roman legions before their political development could advance. They did achieve burials in which great accumulations of wealth and the sacrifice of horses prevailed. In this they were much akin to the Scythians. They contented themselves with making gods of their kings whose burial mounds were the objects of veneration rather than the objects of secrecy.

Integration, Selection, Impermanence

We have suggested that a person may find identity through his interactions with others. An individual integrates into his community by accepting and practicing established modes of behavior. How does the practice of suttee establish a framework for individual integration into the group? The question is twofold because it considers those who participate directly and those who participate vicariously. Both participants have a unique function: to support the public ceremonies that reaffirm the place of constancy and tradition in society. Onlooker and active participant must react in a manner that makes the ceremony and its pomp more important than the end result. The act of dying becomes more important than the fact of death.

Consider the burial service for an important Aztec dignitary. The official death notice was followed by an official mourning period, lasting four days. During this period the Aztecs followed a series of prescribed public rituals most of which involved self-inflicted pain. Bloodletting through self-incision was quite common. Ordinarily a hole was poked through the tongue. Sharp thorns were slowly drawn through the tongue. (Many Aztecs kept this hole open permanently using an inserted peg.) Many abstained from food, drink and sex during the entire mourning time. Priests were always celibate, practicing severe forms of asceticism. Excepting the practice of self-torture and asceticism the funeral practice of the Aztec was kin to that of any society. Individuals were drawn together by the tragedy of death in a formal public demonstration of their emotions. The dead Aztec was fitted out in special clothing. Preparations were made to send the deceased to the great beyond. His body was cremated, the burning of the funeral pyre being, in this instance, a public festival. Slaves and concubines went with him as servants. Death for the Aztec required a prescribed rite, one that had an official beginning and end. All citizens were expected to participate. The ceremony brought the people closer physically and spiritually.

Professor George Reisner, excavating the Nubian cemetery of Kerma, hypothesized about the funeral rite of a provincial governor. This ceremony describes the integrative value of suttee. The funeral procession, bearing the body of the governor on a bed, proceeded from the chapel to the tomb. The governor was decked out with his robes, his sword and the symbols of his office that lay by his side. Slaves carried jars of foodstuffs and oils to be placed in the tomb. The women and attendants of the deceased followed the slaves, each carrying some small item. All of them wailed, bereaving the dead leader. The body was placed in the tomb. The human "grave goods" were dispersed to their assigned positions. The officials and priests closed the doors of the tomb as they departed. Outside the mourners waited for the funeral feast to begin. Each of the mourners took up a basket filled with earth and threw it upon the people in the tomb, including those who were still alive. As each mourner emptied his basket he ran back to refill the basket so that very quickly the entire tomb was filled. After their work was completed the burial party sacrificed oxen and then feasted upon the oxen. The acquiescence of those being buried alive, the hurried work of the basket carriers and the posture of the ceremonial officials were all coordinated to insure the success of the royal funeral.

Human beings have an unholy attraction to pain, especially when it is inflicted upon others. Blood and gore are scenes upon which most people can focus their attention with the greatest concentration. A sort of howling mob unity allows one to transcend the ordinary state of life and to blend into the collective consciousness of the moment. The burial of the Ashanti kings of West Africa provided this spectacle of horrors in which the community experienced this transcendent state. When the king died he was buried with all the usual ceremony. Most of his wives were strangled and buried with him. Being strangled and buried with the monarch was deemed almost as great an honor as being king. Imagine the feelings of the onlookers as they watched each woman being choked, the life breath being literally squeezed out of her. How intense the emotion of the crowd must have been. What of those who did the strangling? What of those who were being strangled?

The wives of the king were not alone in this process. Throughout the kingdom, in every town, slaves, criminals and strangers were sacrificed as funeral offerings. Imagine the sense of community as the townspeople dragged the unfortunate victims to the place of execution. Perhaps individual tribesmen would compete for the right to strangle the first victim. The sense of power over life and death must have been euphoric. All was done in the name and honor of some dead king. An event analogous to this rite might be seen in accounts of the Terror during the French Revolution in which commoners cheered whenever an aristocrat was sent to the guillotine. One can read a chilling description of this in the novel by Anatole France, <u>Les Dieux ont Soif</u>.

The most important factor in the integration of individuals into a community is their recognition of authority. Suttee provided a symbol of the power of the state over its citizens. The king himself was not immune, in some cases, from that very power. The Shilluk kings, who reigned in the Sudan, were chosen every seven years. The former ruler was killed by strangulation at the order of the priests and the nobles. This was easily accomplished because ordinary people were never allowed to see the king's person. His person was held so sacred that only the nobility could attend him. He was buried with a live virgin to insure the fertility of the fields. This is clearly a case in which the upper classes used their position to control the common folks. The awe and majesty in which the king was held and the regular manner of his death served to direct individuals into collective patterns of behavior.

Those who were close to the seat of power often established a community with the leader that made them feel a special solidarity with their group. This was very true among warrior cults. The Natchez Indians vied with one another to be chosen for burial with their chief. The Celts did likewise. Caesar says that the Celts attached themselves to friends with whom they shared all victory and defeat. Each swore an oath to the other that when one died the other should perish as well. According to reports given to Caesar this bond was quite strong as no one could recount anyone who ever broke his pledge. In some instances the relatives of the deceased made the burial arrangements. The Yoruba, Dahomey and Ashanti tribes of West Africa all buried their kings with human grave goods. These were usually war captives killed by strangulation. The relatives of the deceased did the killing, a turnabout from those instances in which the relatives were the victims.

As long as there existed a power figure that could command unswerving loyalty suttee could operate as an integrative function. As time passed and civilizations became more complex the practice generally declined. The reasons are probably more economic than religious. Why waste a perfectly good servant at a funeral? While it lasted suttee did serve in many ways to integrate small communities so that each person might have a suitable ceremony upon which to express his religious devotion.

Not all groups practiced suttee. The problem of cultural selection is more difficult. What factors would cause the selection of this rite as a cultural choice? That fact that there are a limited number of instances among different cultures suggests that the rite was not long popular in any particular setting. The fact that it was mostly limited to royalty suggests that monarchical disposition was required. There is some evidence at Ur that the royal dynasty was overthrown because of popular dissatisfaction with the rulers. Suttee may well have been one of the precipitators of the royal downfall. Few monarchs have controlled the obedience of their subjects so completely that the commoners would voluntarily follow the monarch into death.  I would suggest that suttee, like human sacrifice, represented an offering unlike other offerings. One's own life is the ultimate sacrifice, the ultimate measure of one's devotion. In every time there have always been those who would give up their lives for some great cause. As the power of monarchy declined, at least in absolutist terms, and the value of human life increased, at least in prosperous times, the idea of suttee became less of a cultural option and more of a personal commitment. Eventually the human grave goods were replaced by pictorial representations carved on the walls of tombs.

Suttee is most importantly an expression of the problem of impermanence. In chapter one we stated that the problem of impermanence creates a speculative posture toward death. People want to think of death as a transition to another mode of existence. The whole idea behind burial is the idea of an after life. Suttee represents an attempt to determine the conditions of that afterlife, to insure beforehand that certain proprieties would be observed. Social and political circumstances should be observed in the nether world as they were in the here and now. Much of the ritual involved in these burials was arranged to reinforce that notion.

Consider the position of the king. He did not want to abandon his royal prerogatives. The royal tombs at Abydos, circa 3500 BC, were built to resemble a house. The structure was similar to the palace in which the king had lived. The king's tomb, a kind of throne room, was set in the middle of the burial site. Around this central sarcophagus all of the smaller tombs were arranged. The smaller tombs were those of the servants who had been killed during the king's funeral service. The position of the king in the burial was given deference to insure his continued power in the afterlife. The Scythian and Sumerian kings were likewise buried in special chambers, their attendants usually being buried in lesser chambers to show a status inferior to the monarch. There is in this an almost megalomaniac need to be set apart and above others, to find a sense of security. Perhaps the fear of losing position was one of the principal motivations for suttee. "Even when I die I will have power over my subjects." An early Chinese chronicle states that a Japanese queen, Piminko, circa 238 BC, was buried with one hundred male and female attendants. The queen had been a sorceress in life, supposedly gaining great and dark powers over the people. It was for this reason that she had been elevated to the throne. She was widely feared. In death she sought to maintain her power by taking her servants with her. She presumably entertained the notion that she would continue to practice these dark powers on the other side of the veil.

Among the Tarascans, a pre-Columbian people of Meso-America, a dead king was cremated. His ashes were buried in front of a great temple pyramid, one that was constructed for worship to the gods. His wife and servants were killed and buried behind the pyramid. This was an ordinary custom, confirmed by archeology. The king was given special preference here, his wife and attendants being put in the background. The Meso-American cultures centered their religious and social life in the shadow of their pyramids. Many of the services began at the first step of the stairway leading toward the top of the pyramid.

This is exactly where an important monarch would want to be buried so that he could "supervise" the festivities.

The king's fear of losing his position must have been tied to the fear of being alone, another facet of megalomania. In death the king had the consolation of companions. Misery loves company. The Mycenean king took great pains to prepare for his transition. He had constructed a large stone grave pit. When he died, he was interred with all the treasures accumulated in his life. Food, water and other daily necessities were placed in the grave to give him sustenance. His wife and servants were buried with him so that, among other things, he would not be lonely. The Temple of Inscriptions at Palenque in Meso-America was a temple pyramid constructed around 633 AD. In 1952 excavators found a skeleton, apparently that of an important official, surrounded by a retinue of human skeletons. These attendants were obviously killed at the time of the burial. (The crypt underneath the pyramid is unusual. Until its discovery archeologists believed that pyramids were used exclusively for religious ceremonies and had no funeral function.)

The leader turned his considerations to the demands of utility after his position and companionship had been assured. If the after life were similar to the present he would need servants. Many of the Inca aristocrats, who were not accustomed to doing anything menial, were buried with their attendants. These servants usually included concubines who would, no doubt, serve their masters as before. Fiji chieftains had an interesting variation of this process. Their wives followed them. The luckless females were either strangled or buried alive. Sometimes the mother in law of the chief was also interred in this fashion Menial functions which might need to be performed made utility an important factor. At El Tahin, in the Vera Cruz culture of the Mayas, all of the servants were interred with the deceased. Each female servant was provided with a grinding instrument to grind the master's corn. The Muisca, neighbors of the Maya, believed that the present and after lives were exactly the same. They were buried with all of their wives and servants so that each social stratum might be properly maintained. The

Manta and Canri peoples of Ecuador maintained this same belief, burying their ranking people with wives, servants and utilitarian grave goods. The notion of utility was simply a place for each person and each person in his place. Tasks were not to cease just because death had interrupted the daily routine. Rather servitude would continue in a New World.

## The Question of Esteem

It has been argued that suttee implies recognition of the cycles of nature, of the fact of birth, death and rebirth. Man is simply part of a cosmic whole in which he passes through the same phases of existence as any other living thing. This view of life was particularly strong in the Orient and remains so to the present. The belief in reincarnation was an effective resolution of the problem of impermanence. The notion is acceptable to some degree as an explanation for individual practices such as the Indian woman who threw herself on the funeral pyre of her husband. They do not explain the massive burials of the Shang or other, similar, burials.

These larger burials are clearly a function of power, a measure of self-assurance and a tribute to the self-esteem of individuals. If the soul is going to return to earth it should have no need of companions in the nether world. The megalomania of individuals, not the cultural needs of an entire people, determined the development of this rite. Yet the practice, being selected, became a function of culture. We must admit, however, that aristocratic or royal prerogative is based upon evolutionary cultural developments. The abuse of that power, to satisfy the need for esteem, was responsible for the continuity of the practice through generations. As Buddha once remarked, "He who would seek power and fame is like a child who sucks honey from the blade of a knife. He is only bound to cause suffering."

# 3

## *Ambrosia for the Gods*

Toward the end of the seventh century BC, while the kings of Ur slept unmolested and unknown in their royal graves, the good citizens of Mesopotamia fell upon hard times. War and disease, pestilence and poverty were the gifts of their new and cruel masters. The gods, also, had changed, becoming more bellicose and ruthless. The gentle, pastoral peoples of the Tigris Euphrates had been forsaken by their kindly god king shepherds and abandoned to the lords of war. (Mesopotamia, being a fertile valley as well as a crossroads for civilization, was invaded many times in its long and turbulent history.)

Among these warlords was the Assyrian monarch Assurbanipal, famous for building a great library at Nineveh. The king was concerned with the impiety of the people, thinking that their irresolute sacrileges toward his gods were offensive to heaven. Thus, in the name of his gods, he smote mighty Babylon, and other cities, with his sword. Ur at this time was almost forgotten except for a few temple priests. In this act he believed himself to be assisted by guardian spirits including that of his grandfather, Sennacherib. In the name of these spirits, as a funereal offering to his grandfather and as an amelioration of the anger of the gods he liquidated the populace of Babylon. The bodies of the people were fed to the dogs and pigs. The remains of that feast were left to the disposition of eagles and vultures. When these deeds had appeased the anger of the great gods, the king took the bones of the vanquished and cast them out of the cities. His desire was that he might purify their streets and return the dwellings of the gods to a place of holiness. Babylon became the holy city of Assurbanipal's gods, not those of Babylon. The Babylonian gods and people were considered the enemies of Assurbanipal's gods. It was for this reason that Babylon and its gods were purged, as an offering of atonement for the sins of men.

Although they lived perhaps twelve hundred years after Assurbanipal's Assyrians, the Mayas of Meso-America were equal to the task of dealing with the unfortunates of war. Their practices were a mixture of sexual, religious and cannibal themes. The victim was dragged out to the place of execution. (The Mayas did not practice a wholesale slaughter because their techniques were more refined.) His body was painted blue with dye made from a local plant. Next he was bound and laid out before the image of an idol. The officiating priest picked up an obsidian knife and ceremoniously cut into the sexual parts of the victim. As the blood spurted out the priest gathered the gushing liquid into his hands, turned and smeared the blood on the face of the idol. By now the victim was in intense pain, the life-blood flowing swiftly out of him. Very deftly the priest slipped his knife along the chest of the victim making a deep incision on the left side. Then, as it was still pumping, the heart was ripped out, raised to the idol and rubbed against the stone face of the god as a votive offering.

If the victim was known to be a noble and worthy warrior his body was taken away for further preparation. The women carved the victim as they would a wild beast and then cooked him. This dish was served to the Maya warrior nobility. The feast, which marked the official end of the ceremony, was meant to provide the warriors with the strength of the victim. This method was not the only Maya technique. Occasionally the victim was brought out and tied to a stake. The priest painted a target on the victim's chest, something akin to a bull's eye. The warriors alternated shooting arrows into the target until the victim had expired. In that way the warriors could reaffirm, through demonstration of their prowess in the use of arms, their devotion to the gods.

The Celts, who lived before the Assyrians and remained after the Mayas, had a somewhat different ritual. These nomads worshipped their gods in sacred oak groves. Among the pantheon of Celtic deities were gods with such Roman sounding names as Teutates, Taranis and Esus. Priests called druids served these idols. The druids were thought to be very wise, the word druid meaning Oak Knower. They practiced divination and augury. Their influence was felt from Galatia to Britain. Their victims were dragged into the sacred grove, bound with a special cord and then executed in accord with the religious prescriptions of the god being honored. Some were hung from the branches of the sacred trees. If the head alone were brought to the grove it was nailed to the trunk of a tree. Others were butchered. Their bodies were burned on great funeral pyres.

Occasionally, to mollify the earth gods, victims were thrown into a sacred spring. The number of victims apparently depended upon the number available. Caesar reported that the victims were usually war captives but the Celts, in the absence of any such trophies of war, used members of their own tribe. That they considered this business very seriously is indicated by the Celtic attitude toward inner tribal discipline. Anyone who was out of favor in the community was not allowed to participate in these services. This ousting was considered to be the highest form of social disdain. Tribal members who were so excluded were avoided like the plague.

These three illustrations describe a practice that may well be as ancient as are human beings. Like suttee, the ways of human sacrifice are many and varied, the underlying reasons legion. The practice is generally divided into two types, votive and convivial. Votive sacrifice is simply an offering to a supernatural being for some reason, much like prayer. The offering is made for the benefit of the god alone.

One common type was the sacrifice of prisoners of war. This sacrifice was made to the god of victory in thanks for a successful battle. Convivial sacrifice is one in which the worshiper and the god share the sacrifice in common. The example of the Mayas is such a sacrifice.

They offered the blood and heart of their victim to the god and then ate the rest of the victim as their part of the sacrificial meal.

Freud believed that animal, or human, sacrifice represented a sense of kinship between a group and its god in which both parties shared a common feast. This feasting, which under ordinary circumstances would have been a totem violation and therefore Taboo, was an expression of collective responsibility for, as well as a cathartic release from, what would ordinarily be a severe social restriction. There is in this a very deep sense of belonging to and participating in a social organization. He is really suggesting that human sacrifice, as ritual killing, is a means to vent hostile social feelings in an acceptable way. He is also implying that the individual guilt for such actions is washed away in the collective responsibility for its occurrence. The rest of the chapter will consider the integrating phenomenon, this as a representation of individual identity.

Over the millenniums of human existence there have been countless cults that practiced human sacrifice. To attempt to recount all of them would be sheer folly. This chapter will consider a number of examples in which the rite will be explained in terms of integration, cultural selection and the problem of impermanence, taking into account the question of esteem. In six general categories, which are certainly not inclusive, we shall attempt to illustrate the significance of the rite. Each section will be considered as a complete unit with a summary and explanation to avoid making the chapter simply a long and tedious list of illustrations.

A few comments about the nature of sacrifice are in order. Men have long made perennial and elaborate obeisance to their gods. There is hardly any manufactured or natural article, or any animal or plant used by man, which has not at one time or another been used as a gift to the gods. Sacrifice represents man's willingness to part with something of value in exchange for favors from the deity. Human sacrifice is the ultimate offering of man's possessions. When no other, lesser object, will do the penultimate gift becomes his very life. For what reason does he offer his most valued possession? For what is life exchanged?

The three most important motivations for human sacrifice are the three most basic human motivations, fear, greed and gratitude. Fear is the primary mover when things go wrong. When the crops fail, the plague decimates the populace and barbarian hordes gather at the gate something is wrong. The people have offended the gods either by an act of commission or one of omission. In retaliation the gods have punished the people for their impiety. Many human sacrifices were an attempt to propitiate the ire of the god. Often a scapegoat was chosen for this role. The Phoenicians sacrificed the general who lost an important battle. He had obviously lost favor with the divine. If that sacrifice were not sufficient they would send the children of the nobility into the sacrificial fires. These rites were instituted on a regular basis to insure the divine favor. The Celts sacrificed to their gods if they were ailing or before they went into battle. If they did not offer sacrifice they vowed to do so at a later time.

Greed is as timeless a motivation as fear. The man who has the gods on his side could want for nothing. Most deities were believed to be at war with one another. Certainly the Greek gods were so described. They favored those supporters who rallied to their cause. Riches, power and good health were the putative rewards for loyalty. There are even many references in the bible in which Yahweh caused a man to prosper because of his loyalty. There is a long list including, Noah, Abraham, Job and Moses.

Gratitude is a similar circumstance. Many of the victory celebrations of the warrior nations were designed to show appreciation for favors received. The Thracians, who worshipped victory in the guise of a sword, paid homage to their god by wiping the blood of the men they had killed in battle on the sacred sword image. Most of the agricultural peoples of Meso-America performed a harvest festival in which human victims were offered to the gods of the earth in gratitude for good harvest and for their continued benevolence with future harvests. Of all the tokens of esteem human sacrificial victims are probably the most obvious. Man has made gods to satisfy his own need for an explanation of what he can not understand and then offered to those creations the best of himself.

In no other way are the folly of men and the power of their institutions more aptly demonstrated. Many of the nations who practiced human sacrifice were representative of cultures espousing war. Many sacrificed their prisoners of war. Sometimes these offerings were made in celebration of victory. The ritual became an escape valve for all accumulated blood lust. Often the very object of war was to acquire such victims. This does not suggest that all sacrifices were made immediately after battle or that all prisoners of war were killed in this manner. Some were not killed.

The Aztecs of Mexico were among those most representative of the warrior cult. Originally they were a nomadic group wandering through the valleys of Mexico, conquering and subjugating a variety of tribes. Not until the century before the advent of the Spanish conquistadors had the Aztecs developed a firm control over their empire, a fact that was to contribute to their ultimate defeat by a much smaller military force. The Aztecs favored a military caste system that fostered citizen soldiers. Among the Aztecs the chief aim of battle was the capture of prisoners. This is an important point! The aim of warfare was not to destroy the enemy or disrupt his way of life. War was simply a means toward the acquisition of prisoners for sacrifice. An Aztec military expedition was a harvesting venture in which the chief collected the necessary crops to offer to the gods. The Aztecs had no sense of killing for the sake of killing. This was another fact that made the Spanish conquest so easy. Aztecs could not abide blood lust on the battlefield or as an individual indulgence.

War was the main avenue of the social climber. A humble warrior won great prestige and honor by increasing the number of live captives he brought to the chief. The rewards for such service included a higher position in Aztec society. Offices of state, grants of land and honorary titles were the compensation for dutiful public service. A man could enhance the prestige and position of his family with such accomplishments. The extended family, as a clan, was the basic social unit of the Aztecs. As the sponsor of the individual, the clan received the spoils of war. The greater the participation of the individual the greater share of the bounties of war to his family.

The most demonstrative illustration of the motivation behind Aztec military adventures is an example from the fifteenth century. In 1486, Ahuitzotl, the chief Aztec, completed a great temple at Tenochtitlan. The mighty edifice was constructed to honor two deities, the rain god Tlolac and the war god Huitzilopochtl. With his allies, the Aztec chief engaged in a two-year program to capture prisoners of war. These victims were to be offered as a dedication to the gods of the temple. Eventually some twenty thousand captives were secured. Many were probably the tribute of vassal states rather than prisoners of war taken in battle. During the ceremonies of dedication these captives were brought to the steps of the pyramid and lined in two neat rows. The king and his priestly assistants were waiting for them. As each pair of captives stepped forward the king and his assistants cut into their chests so that they could reach into the chest cavity and rip out the heart. These hearts were tossed into a giant stone cauldron that had been specially fabricated for the occasion. It was called the Great Sacrificial Stone although it was really a basin. The diameter of the stone was eight feet. At the end of the ceremony, when all the victims had been killed, the hearts were burned. It is significant that the Aztec chief participated directly in these festivals. He was a hereditary ruler who was considered the pinnacle of Aztec society. The military caste was arranged in the form of a social pyramid, the majority of the "blocks" on the bottom. The chief was the temporal and spiritual leader of the people. He was considered, if not a god, closer to heaven and the sun than any other mortals were. His direct participation was a physical reaffirmation of the entire structure and purpose of Aztec society.

For a warrior society the celebration of victory is most important. War is an enterprise as unpredictable as any in which one might invest. But war is also highly profitable. The profits are sometimes more emotional than material. According to the ancient chronicler Strabo, the Cimbri, a Teutonic tribe, celebrated victory by destroying all the personal property of their enemies. These foes were also killed in a most horrible fashion. The priestesses of the Cimbri lead each captive to a bronze cauldron. The throat of the victim was cut allowing the blood to flow from his bowed neck into the bowl. This blood letting had two functions. First it was a sacrifice to victory. Secondly the priestess sought to divine future events by judging the physical appearance of the blood. The entire scene must have been a ghastly one. Imagine that you are walking through a busy slaughterhouse on a hot summer day!

The Carthaginians were equally devout in victory. They believed themselves to be the faithful and only servants of Baal Hammon. Their sacrifices were designed to seal the covenant between themselves and their god. The blood of the victims affirmed this bond. For this reason Hannibal executed some three thousand Greek prisoners after the battle of Himera. Other Carthaginian generals, when they were not themselves the victims of sacrifice, followed a similar practice.

In his Annals, Tacitus gave a very graphic description of the fate of Roman prisoners of war that were captured by the Celts. He describes the battleground where the barbarian Arminius defeated the Roman general Quintilius Varus. The account is taken from a first hand observation of the scene recounted some four years after the battle had taken place. Bones of Roman soldiers were strewn about the area where their owners had fallen. Numerous Roman skulls were nailed to tree trunks along with weapons and other military gear. In the nearby sacred grove the Celts had set up sacred altars and offered the tribunes and senior centurions to their gods. It appeared to Tacitus that this was an ordinary custom among the barbarians. His description of the battle field scene suggests that he had encountered nothing that he did not expect to see.

An identical conclusion was drawn by Seutonius Paulinus in 61 AD. At the time he was the Roman military commander of Britain. He undertook the destruction of the sacred groves of the druids. This was done because Paulinus considered them to be a military threat. The druids and their religion required that the altars be soaked with the blood of war captives. Paulinus reported that the druids practiced divination with these war prisoners, trying to ascertain the will of the gods. The priests were known to eviscerate captives and examine their entrails, hoping to spy some sign from the gods. As long as these groves stood Paulinus feared that the priests would be a focal point of rebellion for all the Celts in Britain.

Tacitus described another Germanic tribe, the Hermanduri, who defeated a neighboring rival, the Chatti, in 58 AD. What is curious about this summer victory is that both tribes had sworn the lives of their enemies as an offering to the gods Mercury and Mars. The defeated Chatti were put to the sword. All of their goods were destroyed. Pledging the lives of an enemy in exchange for victory was a common theme among the barbarians. War captives, the most difficult prizes to win, were the most esteemed by the gods.

Greek history provides an incident of human sacrifice. This event was supposed to have occurred before the battle of Salamis in which Themistocles, the Athenian champion, was to match his navel forces against those of Xerxes, the mighty Persian king. (Readers may be more familiar with the famous land battle of this war in which the Greek forces met and defeated the Persians on the plains of Marathon.) Before the battle, Themistocles offered sacrifice to the gods. One Euphramtides, a prophet and soothsayer, saw a vision in which three young Persian nobles were surrounded by flames. At that moment they were prisoners of the Greeks. He brought these three youths before the people and demanded that they be made a sacrifice. Themistocles and other right minded Greeks were shocked and pleaded with the populace not to commit such a dastardly act. But the three were sacrificed to Dionysus, the Flesh Eater, as a votive offering for victory.

This story is from Plutarch. Herodotus, who was well known for his own horror stories, does not mention the tale. He may have been too much of a Greek to make such an admission of fact. The story does suggest the possibility of human sacrifice in the dark ages of Greece. In that era the Greeks were very similar to the Thracians. Plutarch, of course, wrote much later than Herodotus and used a secondary source, Phanias of Lesbos. Herodotus wrote most of his accounts from what he had heard. His contacts with soldiers who were actual participants in the Persian wars seem to make his accounts closer to actual events. In any event, the practice was not unknown in those times. Titus Livy says that the Romans, when threatened with disaster from without, sometimes buried war captives alive as an appeasement to the gods.

Perhaps the method is more important than the actor is. The Mochicha of South America, contemporary with the Incas, threw their war captives from a high cliff. This offering was to the feline deity of their culture. Many groups in Meso-America worshiped the Jaguar as a god, that animal being populous in the jungle regions. The Mochicha severed the arms, legs and genitals of their victims as trophies before the actual defenestration.

The Scythians selected every hundredth man from the ranks of prisoners. These were killed while the remainder of the group was saved for the slave trade. As in the ritual among the Cimbri, the Scythian priests poured wined over the heads of their victims and cut their throats. The blood flowed into a bowl which, when filled, was carried by the priest to the sacred sword and poured out over the hilt and blade. The bodies of the slain were then taken aside so that the right hand and then the right arm might be severed. These parts were ceremoniously tossed into the air and then thrown aside, soon to be part of a disregarded pile of debris. Among the Teutones, a Germanic tribe, sacrifice was accomplished by hanging the victims. Each was swung from a tree in the sacred grove. The rites were performed in honor of Odin who, although immortal, had once swung himself from such a tree for nine days to acquire certain of its magical powers. Or so the Teutones believed. These sacrifices were always carried out in the sacred grove and were followed by a communal feast.

The Aztec fire sacrifice has an interesting twist. This ritual consisted of a number of war captives who were bound and trussed. They were arranged around a great ceremonial fire. Some of the priests held the prisoners in place. Other priests danced around this fire, which had been allowed to settle into burning embers. The captives were thrown into the burning coals and roasted until they were almost dead. Their seared bodies were pulled out. The priest cut into their chests and ripped out their hearts. This was done in honor of Heuheuteotl, the Aztec god of fire.

Another Aztec Ceremony was the gladiator sacrifice. The victim was chosen for his great bravery as a warrior. His body was tied to a stone disc in such a manner as to allow his arms free movement. The priest gave him a club with which to defend himself. Two Aztec warriors set upon him with their weapons. If the victim fought well and kept his opponents at bay he was sometimes released and allowed to join the warrior cult. If unlucky in the contest he became another sacrificial offering. Often the club that was given to the victim was not a real club but only a harmless toy. In that instance he was suppose to appear as though he was fighting. This ruse was for the benefit of the god. This victim was always killed.

The Aztecs also played a ball game something similar to modern basketball, except they could not use their hands. The games were played in specially constructed courts in the temple so that the officiating god could look on. The captain of the losing team was often put to death as an offering of victory to the gods. Hays, in his book, In the Beginnings, suggested that teams represented, vicariously, opposing armies, the loser being offered up by the victor. Many of these games, and subsequent sacrifices, might have taken place in times when there were no wars. In this way they might represent a training exercise in which the real stakes of war, life and death, were put on the line. Under Montezuma I the Tenochos, or Mexico City Aztecs, were encouraged to play these games. The contest was called the War of the Flowers. In this instance the winners sacrificed the losing team to the gods. Montezuma's reasoning was predicated upon economic factors. If the warriors were kept busy fighting, while avoiding a real war, the peacetime economy would not be impaired.

In <u>Tristes Tropiques</u>, Claude Levi-Strauss described a special circumstance in which the killing of the enemy in battle was done, not for the gods, but for men. Among the Tupi Kawahib of the Amazon, a woman and her husband adopted a new name each time the husband killed a prisoner of war. Upon his first kill a young man was given his first name, an appellation which acted within the family group as a function of solidarity.

The killing of war captives as an offering to the gods is largely a function of integration. As a youth approached manhood his preparations for war, which had been going on for some time, became more and more serious. The act of killing prisoners most probably was a training exhibition for those who would be expected to do so in their own time. The Scythians excluded from their public sacrifices all that had not killed a man in battle. To kill was to be made an integral part of the group and to find personal and social communion with the divine. The Aztecs killed thousands of people in their sacrifices each year. Yet there was a close affinity between the captive-victim and the captor-executioner. A kind of professional pride at being either a captive or a captor provided a bond through which both parties could enter into a voluntary participation. Captive prisoners might have thought of death as a duty.

The integration was not, however, simply for the warrior. These sacrifices were usually public spectacles that demonstrated the power and authority of the state, however primitive, over its citizens. In this sense there was chauvinistic pressure put upon women, perhaps to keep them in their place. It must be said that certain peoples, such as the Thracians and the Scythians, encouraged young women to join in the wars and to kill in battle before they settled down to marriage. This is ostensibly the source for the legend of Amazon women who fascinated the classic Greeks.

As far as cultural selection is concerned, killing goes hand in hand with war. After 1000 BC, the Toltecs took over public ceremonies from their priests, thus making sacrifice the responsibility of the warrior caste. This political military coup changed the incidence of human sacrifice in the post-classical period in Meso-America. The brutality and carnage of the act increased even more with the success of the Aztecs. More victories meant more victims that in turn meant more people to guard. Prisoners, if they escaped, could be a threat to internal security. Doing away with them in public sacrifice was a safe expedient. Also the practice of a public execution or sacrifice tended to keep the recalcitrant within the community from digressing from acceptable modes of behavior.

The problem of impermanence must always be on the mind of a warrior. At any moment he could be called to the great beyond without notice. The notions of places such as Valhalla that cater to the importance of the warrior cult demonstrate the attempts to deal with impermanence. Whatever the society or the men at arms, warriors made obeisance to their own special gods of war from whom they expected a special consideration and a special place when they died. The question of esteem is tied to the feelings of blood lust felt by those who performed the sacrifice. There is nothing more fulfilling to a warrior than to see the physical dissolution of his enemies, especially if he has a part in the dissolution. The final and irrevocable conquest has been made in the sacrifice.

## The Occasions of State

Chapter one briefly described the practice of suttee during the Shang dynasty in China. Shang burials also included human sacrifice. There were numerous grave pits built near the central grave pit of the emperor that date from the same period. The pits were filled with headless skeletons. Excavators discovered the missing heads. They were located in other, similar, pits. The excavators suggested that these remains were those of war prisoners who were sacrificed at the death of the king. They were dispatched for the benefit of gods or ancestors on behalf of the emperor.

The coronation of a Ganda king required the sacrifice of slaves, criminals and even members of the royal household. It was believed that the king's life was prolonged by the sacrifice of one of his official's sons. From the boy's body the skin was flayed to make a whip for the king. From the muscles of the victim's back anklets were made for the king. The mode of sacrifice depended upon the locality and the occasion of the execution. Victims were generally clubbed to death after which their bodies were thrown out to the birds and wild beasts. Some were less fortunate. Their arms and legs were broken so that they could not escape the crocodiles for which they had been set out. Royal princes were sacrificed by forced strangulation. These sacrifices were made to the gods and to dead kings who were thought to be gods.

The ancient Persians practiced a vicarious style of ritual regicide. A prisoner was brought to the chamber of the king. He was installed in the king's place, attired in the king's wardrobe and given access to all of the privileges of the monarch. These included his access to the king's harem. Lavishly treated by the king and peers of the realm, the prisoner was placed in a position of great honor. After a few days of this luxurious living he was taken away and summarily put to death.

Among the people of Malekula there was a titular position which gave one the right to wear the great crown, a kind of chief of the chiefs position. Those who sought this honor were called **strivers after the great crown**. These applicants were required to make sacrifice that they might find favor with the gods. The usual sacrifice was a boar, boar being kept and bred for that purpose. Sometimes the striver after the great crown offered a human instead of a boar. The humans were also kept and bred for sacrifice. They were treated with great generosity and affection but were kept happily ignorant of their fate. When their time arrived, the official priest of the sacrifice, who was called the Lord of the Underworld, hung the victim over a dolmen (stone table) and clubbed him to death.

The preceding examples are those of human sacrifice performed on state occasions. They characteristically involved the principal activities of the government, such as a coronation, the opening of a war or some other public and official occasion. Vercingetorix, the great Gallic warrior, was dragged through the streets of Rome behind the chariot of Julius Caesar before the Gaul was put to death. These sacrifices demonstrate the relative position of people within the state and sanctify the importance of official ceremony. The more important the ceremony the more costly the nature of the victim. The Tahitians ordinarily sacrificed dogs and pigs to their gods. On very important religious occasions the ceremony included human sacrifice.

Human sacrifice was a method that the king used to exhibit his supreme power over subjects. Diodorus Siculus provides an interesting example. Diegylis, King of the Caeni, a Thracian tribe, declared to his people that his offerings to the gods must be different from those of ordinary men. He adorned two captured Greek soldiers, by putting garlands on their heads, and slew them with his sword. As he did this his own men stood around him singing a paean (song of praise) to their king.

The Kwakiutl Indians were famous for potlatches in which they tried to outdo one another in the destruction of their own property. If one chief burned his blanket, the other would burn two blankets. If one destroyed cookware, the other would destroy twice as much. The object was to demonstrate how wealthy one was by destroying more property than the opponent destroys. This could amount to an enormous expenditure of wealth. When matters became very serious in these potlatches the chiefs would begin to kill their slaves just to show their indifference to property. Yet this was an acceptable and desirable practice among the Kwakiutl. See Ruth Benedict in Patterns of Culture.

When the Celts decided to wage war they called a general muster of warriors. This was an important state occasion. All adult males were, by common law, required to attend. The last to arrive was put to death. Admittedly an act of simple butchery, this practice illustrates the power of the state to impose ritual killing as a mark of its power. See Caesar, Gallic Wars.

At the elevation on the new Ganda king two foreigners, captured by his soldiers, were brought before the king. One was wounded, taken to the border of the kingdom and left to die. The other was taken to a sacrificial area where he was made to witness the evisceration of eight men. The intestines of the eight were wrapped around the neck of the observer. By this action he became the overseer of the king's wives, he a perfect stranger. The psychological implications of this bizarre practice aside; the power of the king to kill wantonly is clearly demonstrated.

The king was not always so fortunate as to be the object of sacrifice. Sometimes he was the sacrifice. In the temple culture of Zimbabwe the monarch was put to death every four years as part of a perennial sacrifice. His first wife dispatched him. The method was strangulation. After a year went by the favorite wife of the king, not necessarily his first, was stripped naked and strangled. The monarch and his favorite were buried on the side of a mountain, one on the east slope and the other on the west. The king's resting-place was called the Holy Cave. His brain and intestines, which had been removed and stored at the time he was embalmed, were placed with him in great ceremony. Three humans were butchered at the entrance to his gravesite.

Human sacrifice was reserved for the most important occasions among the Inca. The coronation of a new emperor, the start of war or the spreading of an epidemic was such a circumstance. Sacrifice was reserved for only the most important gods. The accession of a new monarch required the sacrifice of two hundred children. These were supposed to be flawless female virgins and about ten years of age. Inca merchants did a brisk trade in the acquisition of such specimens. Sometimes indigent parents sold them. Often they were given as a gesture of reverence for the emperor or out of a sense of duty to the state. No doubt, many of them were simply kidnapped. In the absence of sufficient quantities of the young and flawless, prisoners of war were substituted.

The method of sacrifice among the Inca was in the Aztec fashion. The heart was cut out and offered to the idol of the god. Sometimes the victims were strangled with a cord. Occasionally they were thrown into a sacred well. The method depended upon the god and the occasion. Recently, remains of some of these children have been found, well preserved by the timeless icy mountains of the Andes.

The officials for these state occasions were carefully screened. Only very senior members of the Aztec priesthood were allowed to perform human sacrifices. They were also responsible for the flaying and butchering of the body. The priests were ascetics who spent their entire lives preparing for their stately duties. They abstained from food, drink and sex for inordinate periods to purify themselves for the execution of their holy offices. Confession, self-recrimination and self-torture were fundamental necessities for the practice of their religion.

The Zapotec priests practiced human sacrifice to a lesser degree than did the Aztec priests. The officiating priests were, therefore, of a lower standing in the priesthood. These people butchered dwarves, thought to be sky creatures, in observance of the solar eclipse.

Where the state had power to impose voluntary or involuntary human sacrifice upon its subjects it must have clearly represented itself as an absolute and unyielding power. Such states have been more stratified than one might expect. The integrative function seems less operative because the majority of people have other duties, the duties of sacrifice being relegated to a few hands. Perhaps that is why the practice has become less of a ritual practice and more the art of butchery. A modern example is suggested by the practice of public execution and ritual murder by the Taliban authority in Afghanistan. The religious significance would have come to matter less and less. As states became more complex they became less reliant upon ritual murder as a cohesive factor, less reliant upon any social-political method of cohesion. Cultural options became more and more routine at the same time that they became less and less the progenitors of religious fervor and zeal. As a state occasion human sacrifice became a personal token of esteem.

Cornerstones

The discussion of burial rites in chapter two included a ceremony in which humans were killed and laid within the foundations of temple buildings or funeral monuments. Presumably, this was an effort to strengthen the building by honoring the earth gods. We shall call the victims of these sacrifices "cornerstones". If all public ceremonies within a culture required human sacrifice in order to be dedicated then certainly they would require special victims.

During their La Tene period the Celts were practitioners of this art. When the ancient town of Manching was excavated, archeologists found a thick wall, ten feet high, which had been part of the town fortress. Within this wall lay the skeleton of a six-year old child. This youngster had been offered to the gods to strengthen the wall. Strong walls were an important part of a town's defense. Any ritual that was believed to make those defenses more secure would undoubtedly develop into a regular custom.

Among the Aztecs the burial of individuals under the foundations of buildings was also an offering to the gods. In the cathedral city of Teotihusacan they built a temple to Quezacoatl, one of their principal deities. Excavators found human remains underneath the foundation. The Aztecs were so taken with the idea of killing and of sacrifice that it would be very unlikely that they could have avoided such an opportunity. Their superstition and preoccupation with death almost demanded such an observance.

The Northern Haida of British Columbia practiced this form of sacrifice when they erected a totem pole. A slave was buried in the hole in which their totem pole was to be fixed. When the totem was brought upright into the hole the victim was crushed to death. This was the only form of sacrifice known among the Haida and was practiced infrequently. Within totem cultures distinctions are generally not made between the members of the totem clan and the animal that represents them. One is thought to change into the shape of his totem animal when he dies. The burial of a slave might be thought of as an attempt to satisfy the totem. By feeding the totem its spiritual force might wax strong. The slave, not being a member of the totem clan, would not, of course, be changed into the representative animal.

When the Muisca, neighbors of the Incas, built a palace, they first set up supporting posts for the roof. These posts were sharpened at one end so that they could be driven through the bodies of young girls, probably virgins. Flesh and blood was thought to enhance the strength and durability of a building.

At Woodhenge in England the megalithic builders erected a circle of posts which were thought to be the support beams of a building. In the center of this circle the body of an infant was discovered. This burial was an obvious sacrifice, probably to the earth gods. The infant's skull had been cleft. This site should not be confused with Stonehenge that actually went through three phases of development beginning about the same time as Woodhenge. The remains of similar sacrifices have been found at Stonehenge.

The sources for this topic were extremely limited suggesting that the practice was restricted to the most barbaric of peoples. Although this may not actually be the case, the practice does have a very specialized function, determined by the technology and disposition of the builders. If construction were one of man's most versatile achievements, as it seems to have been among the ancients, then vanity would demand a precious substance with which to consecrate the technological power. Even today we speak often of the value of a great building in terms of how many lives it cost to build.

The integrative function of this practice may have simply served as the opening of construction, the signal for the task to begin. The excitement of "opening ceremonies" might have stimulated the builders and workers and reminded them of the sacred purpose in their charge. Some cathedrals have been constructed in which the relics of a saint were laid as a cornerstone, perhaps a throwback to earlier, more violent rites.

These killings were obvious attempts to deal with the problem of impermanence. The great temples of Mexico were made to last long beyond their owners. The walls of Celtic towns were constructed to protect the people within as well as their descendants. By offering human lives to the gods, the people hoped to improve their own condition. And that is not even to mention the vanity of the men who designed and built them. They were hopeful that these buildings would be a testament through time to their skills.

Scapegoats

In chapter one we made the following point. Cultural preferences for vicarious compensation make human sacrifice an important adjunct of the philosophy, "Take him, not me." The exigencies of the divine might therefore be satisfied on an impersonal or other personal basis. The expurgation of sin and disease might be affected by transmitting these evils to a scapegoat. Consider Dahomey, West Africa, in the 19th century.

The Dahomeans believed that stress situations were signs that the gods were angry. To alleviate that anger they resorted to a scapegoat. The victim was a member of the tribe. Upon his selection he was covered with dust. Next, each member of the tribe touched him. By touching the victim, each tribesman passed his own evil onto the victim. The priest removed the unfortunate man and decapitated him. The Dahomeans believed that the decapitation of the hapless soul removed the evil from him and thereby from the entire tribe.

Among the Inca sin was most often considered the cause of disease. The afflicted was required to confess his sins and to make penance. He might also be expected to make sacrifice to the offended god. This atonement very often required the sacrifice of his very child. The same applied to earthquakes. In Cuzco, the temple of the sun was the principle temple. The Incas believed that this temple was close to the place where earthquakes were born. In order to preclude these disasters the Inca priests sacrificed both children and llamas.

The Navaho Indians of the Western Plains believed that disease was caused by the malevolent practices of a witch. In fact, witchcraft was one of the few crimes for which the Navaho had capital punishment. A special council was called in these cases. Its only duty was to ferret out the witch. Anyone suspected of witchcraft or of practicing the dark powers was required to give testimony to their innocence. If they could not discredit their accusers witches were always put to death. Usually some social pariah was selected and accused to facilitate the duties of the council.

Many of the Pueblo Indians aspired to be sorcerers or shamans. If a man was called by the Water Serpent to practice the dark arts, he was obliged to make offerings to the god. This usually included the death of his wife and children in payment for the future rewards of being a sorcerer. This blessing of the Water Serpent was only for the practice of evil. Such men were considered to be quite dangerous and, in times of stress, were sought out as the cause of misfortune. They were often put to death although the Pueblos believed that sorcerers did not actually die. They merely changed their form.

The Phoenicians also believed in the divine or supernatural cause of sin. In 415 BC, the Carthaginian general, Hannibal, attacked the Greek Town of Selinus. (This was a distant relative of the more famous Hannibal who made war on Rome.) His efforts were successful but he was soon after stricken by disease and died. This epidemic raged through the Carthaginian camp, decimating the ranks. Himilco, Hannibal's successor, decided that the gods were angry. He took a young child, as was the custom among Semitic peoples, and passed the child "through the fire." The sacrifice of atonement was not successful and Himilco was eventually defeated. He went home to Carthage and starved himself to death because he believed that his gods had forsaken him.

Caesar says that the Celts were a very superstitious people and also used scapegoats. They believed that a person suffering from disease must employ the druids to placate the gods on his behalf. Since the only way to save one's life from disease was to offer another life to the gods in exchange, the druids were sought to offer human sacrifice. Regular state sacrifices were held to prevent disease. The druids constructed images that reflected the sacred trees in their grove. These giant wicker edifices were filled with living men and then set on fire to propitiate the gods.

Scapegoats have an obvious integrative function. When life seems to be coming apart at the seams people look for any reason. To accuse and punish someone as being responsible for a group calamity is an easy way to find meaning in a catastrophe. Titus Livy recounts such an incident in his Early History of Rome. The time was 480 BC. The Romans were at war with the Veii, one of their neighbors in Italy. This was before the Romans had secured their position on the Italian Peninsula and long before they set out with their imperial ambitions. The Romans had sufficient military strength to defeat their enemies but they suffered from internal dissension. Many bad omens had been witnessed. The city had a feeling of imminent disaster. The diviners and soothsayers, having made their examinations of entrails and having watched the flights of birds, announced that there had been a serious breech of religious etiquette. The gods were angry about an improper observation of religious ritual. The community needed a scapegoat. A Vestal Virgin named Oppia was accused of having had relations with a man. This lack of chastity was a violation of her religious duties. Livy says the she was put to death, perhaps by being buried alive, and that soon afterward the dissension of the people was dissolved. The tension of the group obviously needed a focal point upon which to release its hostility. The impious Vestal Virgin, who was supposed to be representative of the purity of all Roman women, was a fine target for that ire.

Herodotus tells a tale of Xerxes, the Persian king, and of his Magi which rings a slightly different note. The Magi were the priests of the Persian religion. Responsible for divining portents of the future, they were the chief advisors of the king. At this time, circa 485 BC, the Persians had invaded Greece. Xerxes was marching through Thrace and had come to a river crossing. His priests, hoping to propitiate the river, made preparations to offer sacrifice. At first they sacrificed white horses. Then they crossed the river at a bridge known as the Nine Ways. To make further overtures to the river they buried nine native boys and nine native girls on the bank of the river, these being buried alive. Herodotus says this was an ancient Persian custom. Certainly the act represented an attempt to strike a bargain with the divine by offering something of value.

When Amestris, the wife of Xerxes, was growing old, she gathered fourteen Persian boys from the best of the noble families and had them buried alive. This was an offering to the god of the Nether world. She hoped that the god would accept these presents instead of demanding her own life. Such vicarious sacrifices are clearly designed to deal with the problem of impermanence and the vagaries of fate.

The Carthaginians were conscious of the demands of the divine and of the fickle quality of fate. In 310 BC they were besieged by the Sicilian Agathocles. Their military situation was secure but they were fearful of treachery and the anger of the gods. Sacrifice was made to Baal and Tanit but the situation remained unchanged. Their leaders decided that these religious offerings had been too shallow, their form too inept. They had offered mere slaves to the gods. Now two hundred innocent children were selected for the sacrifice to amend this discrepancy. These were taken from the noblest families in Carthage. Parents volunteered another three hundred to be slain.

All of these examples deal with attempts to overcome disease and calamity. In one sense they are admirable because they show the human mind attempting to gain control over its environment and to determine the outcome of events. On the other hand they represent the apotheosis of the illogic that comes from fear, vanity and greed. But not all scapegoats were chosen to mollify the gods or to eradicate disease and disaster. Some were chosen out of a sense of blood lust or just plain pride.

Among the now extinct Tasmanians, dancing and singing accompanied the killing of an enemy. The group engaged in a ritual mutilation of the enemy body, breaking bones and finger joints. Particular attention was paid to the head. Murdock, who described this phenomenon, did not offer any explanation for this event among the Tasmanians. A group mutilation appears to be an obvious integrative ritual as well as a lesson for the young boys. The practice may have had a politically cohesive effect since the Tasmanians had no permanent chiefs. See George Peter Murdock, Our Primitive Contemporaries.

We have described above the potlatches of the Indians. Those of the Haida and other Northwest tribes were designed to demonstrate the beneficence of the person giving the potlatch. Sometimes a vengeance potlatch was given as a show of contempt for the insult of another. In this ceremony many material goods were destroyed. Among these, as a token of disregard for property, a slave or two might be killed. Slaves were considered to be almost human and might be dispatched in this manner in order to save the face of the injured party.

And then there is the case of Nero Claudius Caesar, known to history as the infamous Nero. After the famous fire that burned parts of Rome, Nero blamed the Christians and made them scapegoats. He ordered them to be dressed in the skins of wild animals. Dogs attacked some. Some were crucified or immolated. The crowning touch was in the palace of the emperor where the Christians were covered with tar and used as torches to light the hallways. Nero could point to these victims and show that they had been brought to justice. Ordinarily one would consider this a simple act of madness on the part of an insane emperor. But Tacitus says that the people supported these actions. They truly believed that the Christians had started the fires. Curiously, Tacitus also believed that the Christians deserved punishment, not for the fire, but for what he called their political and antisocial activities. The Christians, he says, were convicted by the hatred of the public and deserved punishment.

The selection of examples in this section testifies to the universal occurrence of the scapegoat. In a state of anxiety the mind will predicate a cause of trouble however illogical the process of selection becomes. In the case of intercultural contact the choice may result from the extremes of Xenophobia. In the case of inner cultural circumstances someone must be proven to be an alien, if not to the culture, at least to the well being of the group. When people have great trouble they tend to go hunting for monsters. Those who are most eccentric, such as the shaman, may find themselves the object of such an irrational metamorphosis. In times when calamity seems perennial, a culture may adopt a regular public ceremony, such as human sacrifice, to assuage the deities.

Volunteers

Perhaps more fascinating than the fact of human sacrifice is the attitude of the individual. Most citizens of a state would adhere to the necessity of the act were it based upon custom and tradition. Most would also consider themselves immune from the sacrificial knife or fire. At least the chance of their being a victim was slim. But the philosophy "It always happens to the other guy" did not always apply. Some individuals were more than happy to accommodate the whims of the priest executioner.

We have seen the attitude of the Natchez Indians and the Celtic warriors when one of their favorite chiefs died. The warriors vied with one another to determine who would join the chief in death. The Celts even begged to have their throats cut. But this altruistic and suicidal sentimentality is not true human sacrifice. Even those who were volunteers for the Sumerian or Scythian kings were really looking after their own interests. They expected to maintain their position with the monarch. There were some stalwart hearts that gave themselves up as a sacrifice to the gods for the benefit of their fellows.

Such was the aim of the king of Quilcare whose desire was the performance of a ritual self-regicide. He began by assuming a place of prominence in view of all his people. Taking a sharp knife in hand, he cut away parts of his body. Each finger joint was amputated. As each part was cut away he tossed it aside. When his ears, nose, fingers and flesh had been hacked until the blood ran profusely and when he had grown too weak from his task to continue, the king pressed the knife to his throat and slit it side to side. He expired among a throng of cheering onlookers.

In the early history of Egypt, before the building of the pyramids, kings often gave themselves up to this kind of ritual regicide. The cow and bull were early symbols of life and fertility among the peoples who observed regicide, the Earth Mother being the cow and the king representing the bull. As the king grew older he was thought to lose his virile powers and must be replaced by a younger, stronger bull. Sometimes the practice did not wait upon age. If there were a famine or an epidemic the people often blamed the king. He was no longer on good terms with the deity. In this instance he gave himself up to sacrifice for the sake of his kingdom.

A similar circumstance occurred in 1923, in Africa, when a tribal monarch stood up in the center of his people and slowly hacked himself to death. These practices were customary in India and Africa before the coming of Western influence. They represent an intimacy with the cycles of nature and the problem of impermanence. They reflect an attitude toward existence that is as old as are human beings. Sir James George Frazier discussed these rites at length in his book <u>The Golden Bough</u>.

These regicides did not continue long in the cultures where technology and political development raised the king from a religious leader to a purely temporal leader. The priest king became more of a statesman and less of a priest. The ritual regicide was abandoned in favor of vicarious sacrifice. A goat, pig or other animal was substituted. Sometimes the image of the king was used. In one Egyptian ceremony the chief priest slapped the king on both sides of the face as a symbol of his having been killed. Sometimes the king took off his old vestments and put on new ones as a symbol of his rebirth. It became apparent in these cultures that the life of the king was becoming much more important than the ritual of the gods. In those cultures which lacked the development of the monarchical state the practice continued into the twentieth century.

A different form of self-sacrifice was the Roman practice of Devotio. The Roman noble covered his head, offered prayer to the gods and charged into the ranks of the enemy. This wartime sacrifice was common among the Romans and described by Titus Livy. The prayers said were to the gods and the sacrifice of one's life was in exchange for the success of the army in battle. The self-condemned man offered his own life for the glory and victory of his fellows. In the early centuries of the Roman Republic this was the greatest sacrifice which one could make, especially if victory did ensue.

In his history of the mythical Greek King Theseus, Plutarch mentions a similar case. One Marathus, in obeisance to the will of an oracle, allowed himself to be sacrificed to the gods before an important battle. For this feat he was honored by having a town named after him, the city of Marathon. We can not vouch for the verity of Plutarch's story but the implications are real enough in the concept of the sacrificial act.

In his account of the visit of Alexander the Great to India in 327 BC, Strabo, the geographer, reported a different case. In addition to being a military adventurer, Alexander was an amateur historian and philosopher. Wherever this erstwhile student of Aristotle wandered, he sought out the wise men of the land, hoping to learn of their ways and of their wisdom. In India, his scouts discovered a number of such wise persons sitting on hot rocks in the midday sun, naked and oblivious to discomfort. These Indian holy men disdained the dress and manners of the conquering soldiers. Finally one of them, whom the Greeks called Kalanos, consented to meet with the Macedonian and speak about the ways of wisdom.

This man spent some time with the army talking about his beliefs and listening to the descriptions of Greek philosophers. His behavior was not unsettling but very proper; that is until the army was preparing to return to Persia. At that time Kalanos asked the soldiers to build him a funeral pyre. When the structure had been completed he climbed to the top, bade farewell to his friends and burned himself to death. The soldiers of Alexander were mystified by this incredulous act. Campbell suggested that the holy man, as was the custom, had simply changed his existence to a higher form. In his present state he had gone as far toward perfection as he could and therefore must change states in order to advance. This self-effacing attitude was the necessary adjunct of Eastern Philosophy.

The attitude toward life, death and duty is further illustrated by a report made in the year 1813 by a British officer named Kemp. It seems that a certain workman had fallen ill and was told by his astrologer that he was going to die. Accepting this verdict, the man prepared himself by first immersing his body in a mud stream. In that state, accompanied by his friends, he stood for hours patiently awaiting the grim reaper. These immersions were periodically alternated with sunbaths under the hot Indian sun. At the end of thirty hours of this torture, the man did expire, thus confirming what the astrologer had said all along. His wife, a strong and apparently healthy woman, decided that she would join her husband. Being a True Woman she committed herself to being buried with her spouse. This is the original form of suttee discussed in chapter two. At length the man's body was respectfully laid in a pit that was dug by the river. The woman, encouraged by her friends, went into the pit as well, determined and resolute. Nothing the British captain said could dissuade her. She sat patiently as the friends of the couple buried them both.

This is not simply a case of suicide or an observance of nuptial duty brought on by despair. This practice was an ingrained ritual in the people of India, one which continued long and tedious years until finally suppressed by the British. The sacrifice of the self was for a higher nobler purpose. In our own culture we might think of this woman as misdirected, if not insane. In her culture she was regarded as a martyr and a saint. She died for a principle that had been established by her forbears. This principle was an expression of all that was sacred to the people of India. In her reunion with her husband she returned herself to the bosom of the World Soul.

Another example of this self-destruction is taken from the Japanese. Among the nobility, which represented the warrior feudal class, a man who lost face or committed some serious antisocial act was required by custom to kill himself. The procedure warranted a specified number of witnesses whose observations would sanctify the rite. The accused openly admitted his guilt, arranged his body ceremoniously before an altar and cut a zigzag pattern through his intestines, using a dirk. His second, who was also a close personal friend, then cut off the noble's head. This practice was also followed among the Japanese nobility by those retainers of a great lord who wished to join him in death. The accused man might be accompanied by a dozen or more that committed suicide at the same time as he did, even if they were in a distant locale. This practice was outlawed by Japanese authorities as early as the seventeenth century but continued into the twentieth. The Kamikaze pilots of WWII are a good example.

In a society where one is a principal in a dominant caste or party to a sense of spiritual communion with all of nature, the integrative function often relies upon a visible expression of self-sacrifice. The acceptance and glorification of suicide for the benefit of gods or men clearly reflects the process of integration. In the case of the kings who killed themselves, an overt display of the fertility concept and the cycles of death, birth and rebirth are evident. Man, at that level of cultural development, did not make any distinction between himself and the rest of nature. In that respect he was no different from a bird or a flower. That attitude facilitated attempts to deal with the problems of change and impermanence. The Indian woman who dutifully followed her husband into his grave pit did not believe that her existence was to end. It was only changing and perhaps for the better. The kings who hacked themselves to pieces in full view of their subjects were only executing their royal duties and their royal privilege; that is to be at one with the universe.

The situation changes somewhat when we examine the motivation of the Greek, Roman or Japanese military heroes who decided to kill themselves in accordance with some martial code. Perhaps the gods had become equated with the state and the state, becoming ever more powerful, could make greater demands upon the loyalties of its stalwart citizens. Certainly the Roman equestrian and the Japanese Samurai were taken with this idea. The Greeks, being more philosophical and less pragmatic, might have been a trifle recalcitrant in this area. But these people also believed that they were in the process of being transformed rather than obliterated when they consecrated their lives to duty. Perhaps the glory of being remembered as having left the world as a whirlwind instead of as a whimpering sigh was the goal, the price of esteem.

Perennial sacrifice

The title of this chapter is ambrosia for the gods. The exposition of this section will lend some definition to that phrase. From the preceding pages one could suppose that human sacrifice was mostly the act of man bending to the will of the gods. The feeling was genuine. We might say that the gods were merely a cultural reflection of man. To the people who practiced these rites that factor was negligible if it was ever even considered. So the first function of man in his religious life was a votive offering, animal, plant or human, to feed the gods.

The method of feeding or honoring the god was determined by the nature of the god. Let the sacrifice to the rain god involve some ritual using water. The fire god expected some kind of fire ceremony. The earth gods might anticipate live burials as their offerings. Sky gods might expect sacrificial temples to be built. The victim would be closer to the heavens. Many of these factors were determined by geography. A mountain people looked toward the summit for sacrifice. The Semitic peoples who conquered Sumeria built their ziggurats with vegetation along the sides in neat terraces. These were to resemble the mountains of their homeland. The early Thracians, who were close to the Great Mother Goddess, buried their victims in the earth. They lived on flat plains or in valleys. The Celts, who worshipped the fire god, constructed many sacrificial pyres. Celts lived in the forest where there was much kindling. Whatever the method, the rite depended upon the god.

For whatever reason communities needed to have such a dialogue. Perennial sacrifice represented a continuous communication with the divine. A sacrificial victim could be a messenger to the gods. He could also be a surrogate for the god in a convivial sacrifice; an expression of fidelity or simply part of a time honored ceremony serving the integration and solidarity of the group. Very often the gods and sacrifices were used to fix the passing of the seasons. These fostered the community's recognition of the god's role in the cycles of nature. Some examples are in order.

The concept of human sacrifice among the peoples of Meso-America, especially, the Mayans, Toltecs and Aztecs, was related to man's need to seek the favor of the gods. "Feeding" the divine attained this favor. The Aztecs believed that the sun was a god who was in a constant state of motion throughout the day and night. They were ever fearful that the sun god would grow weary in his travels through the nocturnal world and simply remain in the darkness, to rest. Human blood and hearts were offered to nourish him that he might continue his diurnal passage. Man had a duty to keep the sun in the sky so that the plants could grow and the world could flourish. In view of this belief it is easy to see why the Aztecs were so bloodthirsty and had such a strong preoccupation with death.

Sacrificial victims were thought to become stars and were dressed accordingly. They were adorned in sky colored garments bedecked with celestial patterns. War was a holy duty to gain captives that could feed this mighty sun god. The captive was considered to have a great place of honor because he was going to serve the sun god. His death would maintain life on earth.

The typical Aztec human sacrifice was geared to this sun cult. The victim ascended the pyramid, a structure built to insure closer proximity to the sun. The worshipers thronged below. Five priests held him across a sacrificial stone. A sixth priest cut out his heart after cutting into the chest with a sharp knife. The usual material for these tools was obsidian, or volcanic glass. The material is very fragile. When it breaks a clean, razor sharp edge remains. This instrument was ideally suited for cutting flesh. While smearing the blood of the victim on the face of the idol the priest offered the heart to the god. The head was removed for display and the body thrown down the steps of the pyramid. The person who had "sponsored" the victim took the body back to his own domicile. The remains were cooked and eaten by relatives. Compare this to the Christian concept of the Eucharist. The heart was disposed of by burning, fire being a symbol of the sun god.

The Muisca of the Colombian Andes followed the pattern of the Aztecs in believing that human sacrifice was necessary to feed the sun god. Young boys, taken in war, bought from merchants or provided by noble families, were sacrificed in the Aztec fashion. They were usually accepted for sacrifice when they reached puberty. At Guacheta, a young boy was made a victim. This was a weekly event. Warriors used slaves, trussed up in baskets, as targets. They were sacrificed to the god as the spears of the soldiers impaled them.

Further south was the Shipaya tribe of the Amazon who worshipped a god name Kumaphari. This Kumaphari required human flesh from time to time. The local shaman determined the intervals of feeding.

The captive was brought to the village bound with a cord. Until the time of the ritual he was well treated and considered with amity. When his time had arrived he was shot to death with arrows. His body was cut up and boiled. Then the tribe devoured the feast. A small portion was reserved for the god Kumaphari. This was set aside by the river where the god "consumed" his share during the night.

Many of these ceremonies were centered around the cult of the Great Goddess, the earth mother who was representative of the maternal care into which all living things traveled to find their physical and spiritual nurture. Her loyal subjects also must nourish the Earth Mother, as the progenitor of vegetation and animal life. Otherwise nature itself might wither and die. Nowhere was she more evident in her benevolence and in her dark terror than among the Indo-Europeans.

Among the ancient, pre-Homeric Greek field festivals this goddess found staunch supporters. Unlike the Olympiad style worship of later, classical days, these festivities were marked by the sacrifice of humans. Their blood flowed back into the rich womb of their mother, the one who had given them life. So also was the Indian goddess Kali who was pictured as black and timeless. Her necklace was a string of skulls. Her dress was made of the severed appendages of humans. Her tongue was red from the blood of those who had been offered up as sacrifice. Kali was the beginning and end of all things. Every living thing must return to the World Soul, sometimes through Kali. Many of the Indian shrines that exist today have drains that lead into the earth. These were installed years before so that the blood of both human and animal victims might flow more easily into the earth.

Perennial sacrifice involved the belief that the sacrificial victim could be a surrogate for the god. Individual worshipers consumed the flesh and blood of the victim and believed that they were receiving the spirit or mana of the god. The Aztec corn festival included a surrogate of the Corn Goddess. This festival occurred some time after planting when the corn was beginning to show growth. To represent the tender shoots of corn, a girl of tender years was chosen. This maiden was adorned with the dress of the goddess. Her necklace was made of maize cobs. A green feather, representing the green, not yet ripe, tassel of the maize, was her headband. Music and prayer accompanied the festive ceremonies. Nobles struck their fingers with knives to draw blood that they offered to the young girl. At the apex of the ceremony the priest beheaded the young corn maiden and sprinkled her warm blood on the wooden image of the goddess. Her skin was flayed and worn as a vestment by the priest. Her skin was thought to have magic powers as it had functioned as a surrogate for the goddess.

These sacrifices were also designed to elicit special favors from special gods. The Aztec rain gods were honored by human sacrifice. The usual procedure was the drowning of children. Tlaloc was such an Aztec deity. Children were sacrificed to him en mass. The children, who were apparently unaware of what was about to happen, were brought before the altar and encouraged to laugh, play and dance. They were probably rehearsed in this so that their behavior would be acceptable to the god. Then the priests butchered them on a sacrificial stone. Their little hearts were cut out. As all of the children were not killed at the same time, most of them were able to witness what was going to happen. There was a good amount of weeping and crying out. The priests interpreted the weeping as a promise of rain from the god. The louder they cried and the more they wept the more effective the ceremony.

In the Gulf Coast area of North America there was a group of people called the Totonacs. Being agricultural they relied heavily upon the rain god. At three-year intervals they sacrificed a child to the rain god. The participants mixed the blood of the victim with the sap from a tree and drank the concoction. The motivation in this sacrifice was to insure the rain but also to insure the regularity of the rain. In that area, hailstorms and hurricanes are frequent. The principal concern of the Totonacs was to protect the crops from hailstones and cloudbursts.

In Assam, the Durga Puja, or autumn festival, was held in honor of the goddess Kali. The victim, who was supposed to be a volunteer, purified himself. He was dressed in special raiment for the ceremony. He indulged in a lengthy prayer and contemplation and then stood ready for the final offering. His head was cut off and given to Kali. The head was placed on a golden plate. It was believed that this sacrifice, if it were properly performed, would appease the hunger of the goddess. Depending on the victim, the time could be a thousand years and beyond that the goddess was mollified. In the absence of a volunteer the devotees of this cult were not beyond kidnapping a victim.

Among the Pawnee Indians a young girl was selected each year to serve as a planting sacrifice. For six months prior to the ceremony she was treated with great affection and consideration. During the ceremony she was led to each wigwam where she was given a gift of wood and paint. Her body was then painted in two colors, half red and the other half black. Upon the conclusion of this rite she was shot to death with arrows. Her body was cut up into pieces and collected into baskets. Each piece was taken to the field and squeezed over the newly planted cornfields so that the blood would drip upon and nourish the seeds. See E.O. James, The Origin of Sacrifice.

A similar practice was found among the Khonds of India. Their victims were known as Meriah and were acquired by purchase, donation or kidnapping. The Meriah were sometimes kept for years and, in a fashion similar to the Tahitian victims, were often bred with one another to insure a constant supply of victims. Before the ceremony the victim was anointed and shorn of hair. The methods of execution varied with the locale although the end result was the sectioning of the victim into parts. Frazier described the use of revolving wooden elephants upon which the victims were tied. As the mechanical assembly turned the crowd cut strips from the victim until the supply of flesh had been exhausted. Other victims were strangled and then dissected. Each piece of flesh was carried to the village of the man who had acquired the token. In the village the flesh was divided again among the households. The head of each household buried his portion in his own field. This was an offering to the Earth Goddess in hopes of a favorable harvest. In one village fourteen of these wooden elephants were reported suggesting that the practice was extensive.

The sacrificial victim was often a messenger designated to communicate with the gods. The Getae, a people of Thracian origin, believed that one, Zalmoxis, a local hero, had gone before them to prepare a life of unrivaled happiness for the true believers. Their belief placed emphasis upon the transcendent quality of the soul, the body being its mere capsule. They must insure that Zalmoxis remembered them. Every five years they sent a "messenger" to the hero. The choice was made by lottery. Two men swung the victim by the hands and feet to gain sufficient momentum to hurl his body upon three spear points. See Herodotus, Persian Wars.

Money Kyrle quotes Frazer as saying that the people of China's Tang Dynasty married a maiden to the Yellow River each year. The well being of the community depended upon the fertility of the land which in turn hinged upon the river. This sacrifice was most important. Old women selected and dispatched the girl. She was chosen from the most beautiful maidens in the land. Her manner of death was drowning. See Money Kyrle, The Meaning of Sacrifice.

The Wajoggo of German East Africa performed a similar rite with an uncircumcised child. They believed that their ancestors had dwelled within the river and now controlled its flow. This child, thrown into the river, was an offering of propitiation. This ceremony began before the irrigation of the fields.

The Phoenicians also had their messengers. Topeths were constructed to make sacrifice. These were altars built outside and designed to work as an oven. The victim was passed into the fiery oven, as one would place a loaf of bread into a kiln to bake. Archeologists have discovered the charred bones of both animals and humans, the human bones being those of children. These sacrifices were thought to be the highest mark of respect to the gods, a sign that the people had not forgotten their deities. See Gerhard Herm, <u>The Phoenicians, The Purple</u> <u>Empire of the Ancient World</u>.

Perennial observation of human sacrifice extended a religious and time-honored sanction to the various rites discussed in this section. Many became part of the calendar system, especially among the Aztecs. Most Aztec human sacrifices were so fixed, according to the season. The discussion of these rites by Sahugan is truly a calendar of horrors. February 22 was the feast of Tlacaxipeualiztli. Captives were flayed and sacrificed. The flesh was eaten. People who suffered from skin diseases wore the skin of females.

The Aztec calendar was based upon a 52-year cycle at the end of which a new era was begun by human sacrifice. The opening of the ceremony required the generation of a new fire. All old fires were extinguished. The priest used a fire drill to start a new fire on the breast of one of the victims. When the fire was lit the victim's heart was pulled out. His body was allowed to burn as the people gashed themselves in blood sacrifice.

All of these practices served to integrate the individual into his community. In almost every instance participation was mandatory. Whether the rite involved burning the children of nobles, burying the corn maiden or nourishing the sun god, the intent was to establish the relationship of the individual to the group. The group became a holistic expression of its history and culture. The perennial nature of sacrifice made possible the anticipation of events that would secure that holistic expression.

Perennial sacrifice also represents the optimum in cultural selection since only those rites are going to survive that most satisfied the group. This depended greatly upon ecological factors as well as human disposition. The changing cultural posture of the community would effect evolutionary modifications occasionally disrupted by revolutionary influence.

The question of impermanence is also readily accommodated by perennial sacrifice. The mimicry of the cycles of nature suggests a close attachment to the concept of rebirth through imitation and consummation. The apparent indifference to the pain of the victim and the imperative need for "recycling" presupposes that attachment. This is no more obvious than in the fertility rites of the Marind Anim of Dutch South New Guinea. A girl was placed under a platform made of heavy logs, supported by thin poles. Each of the young males was allowed to copulate with the girl, one after another. When the last male had performed this "sacred" act, and while he was still lying with the girl, the poles were kicked away and the couple was crushed by the logs. Their bodies were cooked and eaten.

## The Question of Esteem

Self-perception is a function of many variables most of which are external to the individual. Culture exercises great influence in giving one a sense of purpose and belonging as well as the assurance of having some power over the world. If Alfred Adler was correct in suggesting that the drive for power is a primary impetus then ritual inhumanity makes all the more sense. These practices were an attempt to overcome the environment in some way. The fact that the sacrificial act is totally unrelated to the desired end really makes no difference to the practitioner.

Self-perception demands that life is not unrelenting tragedy. To be unable to affect the course of events would be too brutal a realization. The attempt must be made. Many isolated ethnocentric peoples have resolved the issue by ascribing life to everything in nature. Rocks, water, trees and any other objects must be alive. Death becomes not so much a tragedy as a transition from one condition of energy to another. Acceptance of universal life energy and its translation into different forms gave rise to its use as a social currency. In religion, human sacrifice was a transfer of life energy to the environment and the course of fate. Sustained, the practitioners would not lose their power, the same power through which man hoped to achieve his goals. Obviously if the gods were fed by man through man's own life energy then the self-perception of the individual and the group was enhanced by sacrifice. The final power lay with the benefactors of the gods.

# 4

## *Ornaments*

Most of our discussion has concerned a plethora of seemingly universal social practices. The use of the tokens of esteem were focused upon the acts of being born, coming of age, observing religious practices, making war and dying. This chapter will be no exception to the pattern. Aside from the butchery of human sacrifice the use of human ornaments was the most gruesome of all cultural enterprises. Yet ornamentation has always been an important aspect of social living. The use of human ornaments will prove to have been an integral function for ethnocentric peoples. A few examples will illustrate the point.

The Crow Indians of the Western Plains believed in a sun god. This solar deity was perceived as a protective and beneficent uncle whose main purpose was to grant the requests of his nephews, the Crow warriors. That member of the tribe who wanted a long life or other important favor repaired to the mountains. There, in the seclusion of the god's country, he fasted, taking no food or water or sleep. The rocky ground and inclement weather were supposed to facilitate his communion with the divine. Like many of the world's ascetic petitioners he was supposed to be as uncomfortable as possible. At a propitious moment, perhaps after a vision, he would amputate the first phalange of his left forefinger. This appendage was then proffered to the uncle sun god, a token of esteem. The practice was reserved for males and was apparently connected to a coming of age ceremony.

Childbirth provides a different example. Among the Trobriand Islanders of Melanesia gardening was a principal economic activity.

The crop of yams was especially important as a source of food and as a measure of familial status and worth. Each household kept a plot for this purpose. Special magical incantations were used to guard the plot from enemies. The failure of the crop or a meager harvest was thought to be the work of the enemy of which each Trobriander thought he had many. It is not surprising that newborn children should have a role in protecting and fructifying the family plot. When a child was born, the afterbirth and umbilical cord were saved. These items were taken to the yam garden, in great secrecy, and buried. By this action a psychic link between the garden and the child was established. The garden thus possessed a hold upon the mental attention of the child; a connection that lasted his entire life and bound him to the garden and to the extended family that was responsible for its maintenance.

This was not only a fertility rite meant to insure the harvest. The nexus was designed to make legitimate the birth of the child. Through this rite he was accepted into the community and into the family with all of the rights and responsibilities of a member in his age group. He was expected to fulfill his obligations and to protect the members of his clan from harm, either by physical or magical means. Since these people put great store by the magic of words, the child was expected to learn secret curses and other incantations associated with his garden plot and the relationship that his birth had established.

Body fluids were used in fertility rites. The Flesh of the Pawnee corn maiden and the Khond Meriah were squeezed over the fields, this to add life to the newly sewn grain. The Huancauila of Peru used a fertility rite in which human blood was used to nourish the crops. Blood seems to have been a universal symbol of life energy, a substance whereby health and well being might be transferred from one being to another. Archeologists have unearthed numerous instances of the prehistoric use of blood. Stone Age men used ocher to paint their dead comrades. They hoped to restore them to some semblance of life. Ocher is a red colored iron oxide that was used as a pigment. In his hunting scenes prehistoric man depicted the spot where an animal had been wounded. He also made some connection between fire and blood, the heat and vitality of fire being similar to the warmth and color of blood.

Blood was also perceived as a transfer medium by which one could acquire characteristics. This transfer could be familial or completely impersonal. Warriors who drank the blood of their enemies hoped to acquire the virtue and strength of the defeated. Some communities drank the blood of their own deceased with that idea in mind. Some slash and burn agricultural peoples even went so far as to cremate their dead, mix the ashes with fermented coconut juice and drink the resulting mixture. Others accomplished the same end by simply eating the dead. The transfer of values, especially among small groups, helped to sustain the moral integrity of the people and to enhance their sense of self-preservation.

Keeping spiritual and cultural integrity was important in more developed societies as well. The Romans believed that a father passed his cultural and physical heritage through his blood to his sons, especially to the eldest son. Titus Livy reported that the patricians of Rome were prone to great anxiety over the issue of mixed marriages, that is marriages between noble and commoner. The reason was because the child would not have any idea about his identity or what form of religious worship he should perform. Romans practiced religion in a manner prescribed by their birth and social station. Intermarriage and the mixing of the blood would defile the integrity of the society as well as make impossible a proper relationship between man and the gods. (Ashley Montagu is one of the most outstanding critics of this concept of blood that he says is pure nonsense. There is no genetic power in blood or any way in which cultural traits can be traced to blood. His books on the subject are well worth reading.)

Warfare was another important area for the use of human body parts. Arms, legs, ears, noses and more personal appendages were favorite trophies for the warrior. Because they were symbols of power and virility, the taking of these trophies was effected for any minimal reason. Heads were very popular. Less important parts had their function also. Tacitus gives us a typical example. In 49 AD the Roman favorite for the throne of Parthia was Meherdates. Despite the support of the Romans he lost the battle to his kinsman, Gotarzes. Meherdates was bound and brought before his victorious cousin. Such a trial and judgment would ordinarily mean death. In a demonstration of contempt for Rome and as a sign of his own merciful benevolence Gotarzes freed his captive kinsman after first cutting off his ears. This was a common trait among eastern rulers. Tacitus does not mention what became of the ears but the intent of the act is clear.

The act of dying also had its ornaments. We have mentioned the Manus of Melanesia who preserved the skull of their fathers. Other amulets were preserved as keepsakes of the departed. Some of the circumpolar peoples kept the skeletons of their most important shamans housed in shrines. One of the most bizarre practices occurred among the Muisca, neighbors of the Inca. The bodies of the Muisca kings were mummified. The process included resination, fire drying and probably evisceration. When the taxidermist was finished, the mummy was housed in a special lodge along with others of its kind. When the Muisca went into battle they carried these dead, fire dried kings. The warriors gained added strength from the presence of their departed heroes.

Many of these practices reflect a customary attitude toward the vital processes of life. Indeed, they are attempts to recognize and control those processes. But some were simply expressive of a need to adorn the body with some trinket. Claude Levi-Strauss observed such an expression among the Bororro Indians of South America. The women plucked the temple hair from the men while the men took hair from the head of their wives and braided it into long strands. These strands were wound around their heads in the shape of a turban.

Like human sacrifice, the use of human parts in ritual was very widespread. To attempt to recount every instance would fill libraries. As our study is concerned with the integrative function of these practices we shall hopefully provide those examples which fully illustrate the process whereby the individual deals with the problems of integration, cultural selection and impermanence. These shall be considered as they affected the task of everyday life in different communities. A few words about the nature of human ornamentation are in order.

Unlike human sacrifice, the use of body parts is not always directed toward the heavens. It is true that the Aztecs used the hearts of their victims as an offering to the sun god. Many societies have engaged in general bloodletting to appease their sins and their gods. Yet much of ornamentation is designed strictly for terrestrial use, body parts being the truest form of tokens of esteem. Prestige, personal power and wealth rank along with propitiation, atonement and fear as motivations for these actions.

In most warrior societies the severed head of an enemy brought its owner great esteem within the community along with the opportunity for advancement within the tribe and probably a greater share in the spoils of battle. In less bellicose societies the use of body parts in magic brought the user the same kind of attention. Voodoo, a corruption of the Dahomean Vodu, is an example. Witchcraft or warfare, the result was the same, to bring the individual to the center of attention within his group, to the pinnacle of esteem.

Rite de Naissance

Among most peoples the birth of a child is a great event, usually followed by some ritual recognition and sanctification of the child. The proud father may distribute gifts to his friends as he extols the virtues of his child, the child's prospects for the future and the father's virility. The mother may proudly display her newborn charge throughout the community while constantly fussing over some aspect of his appearance. Grandparents and other relatives are equal participants. By their recognition the circles of family and friends all contribute to the fact of birth. Plans are constructed with the promise of the future.

The advent of a child requires at least three actions on the part of the community. He must be recognized as a member of the group. His membership must be established by ritual. Some provision must be made for his future. Peoples of the past were no different from those of the present in recognizing these social necessities. Their acceptance of the child may have been even more important. Their reliance upon the extended family was much greater than our own. The survival of some groups was so precarious that the development of families was paramount to the future of the culture. The continual development of the clan strengthened the social purpose of the group. The attention and prestige associated with being a new parent was reinforced by ritual. In this manner the child became a link between the past and the future.

Birth rituals were also affected by the high rate of infant mortality. Measures were taken to protect the child from evil spirits and the vicissitudes of fortune. Amulets, charms and incantations were common. Many societies practiced a curious mixture of overprotection and neglect. In good times, when the food supply was regular, the child was a welcome addition to the social structure. In hard times he might be left to die. If his mother died, a child was often buried with her. There was no one else to look after him.

Infanticide, although widely practiced as an economic measure, was not limited to the hard times. The Incas and the Phoenicians sacrificed infants to their gods. More significant were the children born with physiological and anatomical irregularities. Lack of modern medical methods, the close genetic ties within societies and the less than substantive nutrition may have resulted in numerous birth defects. Many of these defects were viewed as signs from the gods or as the work of evil spirits. Most of the children were cast aside. The Incas also sacrificed dwarves, persons analogous to children, to their sun god.

Twins were a special case. Among the Arunta of Australia twins were always considered unnatural and were killed. The Todas of India were more selective. If the twins were boys they were preserved. If they were girls they were killed. If there were a boy and a girl the girl was killed. Among the Ganda twins were accepted with great ritual. The Ganda father observed a special ceremony in which he made a ball from his hair and nail parings. His next task was to kill an enemy and stuff the ball of nail parings and hair into his enemy's mouth. This was probably intended to have some magical effect.

One might say that the attitude and reaction toward twins varied from one group to another according to the group's tolerance for the abnormal. It is important to recognize that twins presented these peoples with special kinds of problems, some of which affect modern man in a more benign way. Three such difficulties are the question of heredity, the relative position of individuals within the community and the problem of identity. Many communities enforced a kind of primogeniture in which only the eldest son could succeed to his father's wealth and position. In communities where a man could become king after his father this was very important. Many twins might have been killed to preclude this problem. Ganda kings killed the first born son so that the son could not grow up to overthrow the father. Killing one or both of the twins may have been designed to establish a precedent for peaceable inheritance. In societies where heredity was matrilineal this factor may not have been considered.

Certain social problems might arise from the fact of twins, especially if they were identical. How were the other members of the community to determine the pecking order of two individuals who seem exactly alike? In our own complex society this question seems absurd but to a small group in an obscure forest it could be very important. Consider the problems of leadership. The story of Romulus and Remus, the mythical founders of Rome, is a good example of how twins can affect the social structure. In trying to establish authority for himself and his followers, Romulus enacted a rule that Remus deliberately broke. The result was fratricide, Romulus killing his brother.

The third problem with twins is the metaphysical one. Could a person truly be whole if he had a living mirror? Was it possible that his soul was divided? The implication of this division could mean that the individual might have trouble in the next world. One reason for the killing of twins might have been to reunite their spirit into one being. Where one was killed the same logic might apply. Inevitably the fate of the twins was determined by the limits of communal tolerance for the irregular.

The well being of the child was often placed in the province of magic. The use of sorcery required parts of the child, parts that had been involved in his birth. The two most obvious and readily available were the placenta and the umbilical cord. The placenta is the membrane by which the fetus is attached to the uterine wall. Ordinarily it is discharged after the baby and is called afterbirth. Ethnocentric people attached great importance to the afterbirth but were unaware of its physiological function. The umbilical cord attaches the fetus to the placenta and acts as a kind of lifeline between the mother and child. Of this there may have been a greater understanding. Childbirth procedures around the world have recognized the necessity for cutting the cord at the time of birth. This fact may have been acquired by instinct or by watching the birthing patterns of other mammals. Dogs, for example, instinctively chew through the umbilical cord and tear the placenta from around the pup. The importance of these body parts in birth rituals will become more evident with the following illustrations.

Acceptance was a primary factor among the Ganda. The child must be proved legitimate to be a member and to adopt his father's name. To determine his merit the Ganda devised a curious test. A container was filled with a mixture of milk, beer and water. The child's umbilical cord was dropped into the mixture. If the cord floated the child was accepted. If it did not float he was considered a bastard. The mother was flogged for infidelity and the grandfather must determine the name of the child.

The magical properties of the umbilical cord were thought to extend beyond the early years of the child. The Ganda kept the umbilical cord of their king in a special place attended by an official called the Kimbugwe. His sole function was to be keeper of the royal umbilical cord.

The cord was believed to be the twin of the king. Periodically the cord was exposed to moonlight and greased with butter. As the Ganda were keepers of cattle it was natural and logical for them to make butter a sacred ointment.

Cords were also preserved for their putative medicinal properties. The Inca preserved the umbilical cords of their children for this purpose. If the child should fall ill during its infancy, the mother would cut off part of the cord and give it to the child to chew. The Crow Indians kept the umbilical cords of females preserved in a special bag. This bag was attached to the back of the infant's dress to act as an amulet. Of course these practices had no effective medical value outside of their potential psychological effect.

The placenta played a ritual role in the well being and the future of the child. The Nootka Indians of British Columbia buried the placenta four days after the birth of the child. The ceremonies associated with this burial were supposed to determine the child's future. Singing songs was supposed to make the child a good singer. Tools buried with the afterbirth would insure the boy was a good artisan. Female afterbirth was generally buried with pieces of basket or cloth to make the girl a good weaver.

The birth of a Tahitian child was also accompanied by the burial of the afterbirth. The umbilical cord was included. The placenta was interred near the Marae. This was a sacred place that the Tahitians associated with their ancestors and their religion. Most public ceremonies and initiation rites were performed on this holy ground. The umbilical cord was buried in a chamber inside the area of the Marae. The Tahitians believed that the navel cord was the essence of the child. Burial within the community's sacred ground connected the child to the culture and gave his soul a place in the spiritual community of Tahiti.

The burial of the placenta and the preservation of the umbilical cord reflected a genuine concern for the life process of the child. The afterbirth, which could not be preserved, was buried as though it was a deceased part of the child. Among the Cheyenne Indians the afterbirth was tied to a tree. They also buried their dead in trees. The Arunta of Australia and the Tungas of Siberia buried the placenta. The Yahagan of Tierra Del Fuego burned the substance. In the same fashion, these peoples preserved the umbilical, an item that was physically constituted and suitable for preservation. The Tungas and the Yahagan saved the cord for its magical properties. The Arunta, and others, used the cord as a necklace for the child. These practices were truly an exercise in sympathetic magic, designed to exert control over the child's life.

Most initiation rites are intended to effect the integration of the individual into his group. In this case the rite de naissance was the first, the entrance step. The child was recognized and accepted as a functional member of the group. The rituals surrounding his birth obviously acted as a focal point through which the group was drawn closer. At the same time his future was planned.

The economy of infanticide and the tragic unpredictability of infant mortality forced the problem of impermanence upon the perception of parents. Although the act of being born and the fact of dying seem to be polar opposites, they are equal parts in the process of being and might even be considered as extensions of one another. To believe that one can, through the employ of sympathetic magic, use human parts to control that process creates a large measure of esteem.

Rite de Passage

Following the initiation of birth the most important event was the rite de passage, the coming of age ceremony. By this ritual the individual was recognized and accepted as an adult member of the community, responsible for obedience to its laws and entitled to its social privileges. These ceremonies have often been confused with fertility rites. Fertility rites are designed for good harvests and animal increase but have little to do directly with the coming of age.

These ceremonies were usually preceded by a period of instruction, indoctrination and testing. The process could be very elaborate. Rituals were learned and practiced. Sacred and secret words were pronounced. A new sense of understanding and meaning was instilled in the young candidates. Passage was a step beyond childhood; one whereby the young man or woman was forever separated from the life that had gone before. For a young boy, ties with the mother were broken. Life became a secret mystery to which only the initiated were introduced and which only the initiated could truly understand.

Admission to the adult community had its price. Tests of endurance and strength were required. Self-torture and scarification were not uncommon. Maiming and dismemberment were popular among some groups. The candidate must prove himself worthy of his quest. Baths in ice water or snow, long hours without sleep or food and a constant sense of self-mortification were the rule. Even flogging and fire branding were practiced. To run the gauntlet was the mark of a true and worthy man. To show no pain was the badge of honor.

These processes required a spiritual obedience. To become a full member of the tribe one had to surrender his will to the tribal leadership. Sometimes he was required to surrender a physical part of himself. Bloodletting was common and often communal. Occasionally the novice was expected to take a part of an enemy's body. Head hunting was a customary form of this practice. As a token of manhood he might receive the body parts of a member of his own tribe. Blood was a frequently used currency in this exchange. The following examples will demonstrate the use of body parts in the coming of age and their effect upon those who paid the purchase price.

One of the most common initiation practices was circumcision. In females this procedure is called excision or clitoridectomy. For women, it was and remains one of the most painful and medically unnecessary surgical acts in the world. Widely practiced today as a measure of health, male circumcision was, in past times, more of a spiritual and social function. For some groups the relationship of circumcision to the body was similar to the relationship between baptism and original sin. The Bambara of the Sudan believed that an evil principle existed in the body, a principle that they called the Wanzo. This Wanzo was thought to dwell in the prepuce of the male and the clitoris of the female. Either circumcision or excision accomplished the exorcism of this evil principle.

All of the young men were circumcised together. They were made to gather around a pit in the earth and allow the blood to drip onto the ground. All of their Wanzo would therefore be collected in one place. A fire ceremony followed in which the Wanzo was joined to that of the previous circumcision ceremony. This sexual division between male and female was prescribed by ritual. The Bambara believed that men and women had both sexual principles inside them. We would say they both have an X chromosome. The process of excision or circumcision removed one of these principles. At the same time the submission to this ritual represented submission to authority of the elders.

The bushmen of the Kalahari exacted the same obedience. In their ritual the little finger of a young boy's right hand was amputated. The right hand was ordinarily used to pull back the bowstring during the hunt, hunting being an adult male occupation. Hays suggested that this amputation represented a kind of ritual castration whereby the older men of the tribe reinforced their power and authority over the younger ones. Among several African tribes this was accomplished by removing one of the testicles from the young man. An apparent connection was made between sexual potency and hunting potency in these rites as well as a nexus between sexual power and physical power. Ritual control over the coming of age would mean social and political control. Access to women of the tribe was often reserved for the older men as a sign of the same authority.

Seniority was recognized among many peoples including the Tariannas of South America. Among these people passage was marked by a ceremony in which all of the old men wore masks. These masked elders whipped the young men. There was a sexual aspect to this as well. The masks were made of monkey hair combined with the hair of young girls who had just achieved menses. The idea was to reinforce the status and power of the older men by ceremoniously making a connection between fertility, menstruation and the old men themselves.

Self-torture was not always a symbol of submission. In the Indian tribes of central North America torture was a preparation for war and a mark of honor. The initiates sought visions through pain. The true warrior cut flesh from his body, hung himself from hooks for hours, amputated some of his fingers, abstained from nourishment for days and dragged heavy objects with ropes attached to hooks planted in his chest. All of this was performed to achieve manhood and its sequel, membership in the war party.

The rite de passage was also a time for creating lasting bonds between individuals and groups. In Africa there were sometimes symbiotic trade relationships between blacks and pygmies. These relationships were based upon the respective occupations of hunting and agriculture. During puberty rites the bonds between the two peoples were cemented. The black and pygmy boys were circumcised at the same time. The blood from both operations was allowed to drip together on the ground. This mixing of blood fused the bond between the two boys for life, making each responsible for the other. Each was obligated to formally lament the other's passing from life. This bond between the two groups was not universally observed in Africa. Where the connection was initiated the bond was very strong.

The circumcision rites of the Arunta had a social aspect similar to the black pygmy symbiosis. The men incised themselves. The boys who received the initiation rites were made to drink this blood so that they would be sustained by it. The blood ritual was supposed to form an attachment between the boy and his father that drew the boy away from maternal ties and brought him into the adult male world.

In the Arunta ceremony the boy also received a belt made of human hair. This belt was the typical dress of the Arunta who wore no other clothing, save for some small decorative items. The belt hair was taken from the boy's father. If the father died before the ceremony could take place, his hair was cut off and saved for the initiation of his son. This hair belt represented a further bond between the father and his son, one which even death could not preclude.

The Tucuna of the Amazon had a similar belief in the bonding properties of hair. They believed that the life force of an individual was located in the hair. When a girl reached menses her hair was pulled out as a symbolic enactment of death. This would presumably grant her long life since death had been ritually satisfied. After her hair had grown back she was accepted as a regular adult member of the tribe.

Although this use of hair may seem puzzling, the practice of attributing life properties to hair and fingernails seems quite logical. These features of the body are ever reproducing themselves. Cut them off and they grow back. When a person dies, his body metabolism stops. His hair and nails will continue to grow for several days after death. It is little wonder then that the Arunta and the Tucuna attributed life properties to hair.

Sometimes the young man was expected to acquire the body parts of his enemy. Head hunting and headhunters will be discussed in the following chapter. We have mentioned that some tribes, such as the Scythians, drank the blood of their enemies, a young man being accepted in the tribe only after he had killed an enemy in battle. The Galla of North East Africa kept a social custom which required a young man to murder before he could advance into the tribal hierarchy. This rite de passage included a task in which the candidate waylaid an enemy and castrated him. The genitals were returned to the village for display. The young man entered manhood and became eligible for marriage. This practice reaffirms the primitive view of the relationship between sexual potency and social importance. Emasculating an enemy or a rival was the same as reducing his status and the threat of his ambitions.

The function of the passage rite was to insure that each new member was acceptable to the tribe, learned the rules of social behavior and submitted to the authority of those in power. Having passed the trial he was given a new identity and place and became an expression of his culture. He was a singular social unit integrated into the whole. Trophies, whether taken from himself, a member of his tribe or from an enemy testified to his new status. The use of human parts was particularly important because they were recognized as being vital to the well being of the body. The nexus was thus made between the individual and the group insuring the vitality and well being of the cultural unit.

The kinds and uses of these practices were many and varied. They depended upon the location and the technological adroitness of the people. The problem of impermanence was confronted by establishing a continuous flow of cultural exchange, from the old to the young, through these initiation rites. Body parts became a symbol of that continuity as well as an immediate expression of esteem.

Fertility, Religion and Magic

Most peoples have been non heroic. That means than an account of their existence is filled with the everyday struggles of survival rather than with adventure stories. Food, shelter and security have been their goals. Not surprisingly the use of magic, religion and fertility rites have been employed to insure the attainment of those very goals. In some societies the use of body parts have played a major role in the achievement of those goals.

Fertility was a primary concern to agricultural peoples. We have seen how some groups would use the flesh or the blood of their sacrificial victims to try to instill some fertility in the soil. The burial of what had been living flesh was expected to generate life in the soil. In some instances the flesh was an offering to the great goddess through whom all things were believed to inevitably pass. The cycles of nature needed to be helped along from time to time by the agriculturists.

Religion, as a source from which people could draw support for their everyday lives, was equally important. As demonstrated in chapter two, human flesh and blood were offered to the gods in return for various favors. The same Pawnee girl who was cut up and thrown into the earth was first offered to the gods. The multitude of Aztec gods who required human parts to feed upon suggests the same importance attached to the gods and the need for religion.

Magic was a special case because it required special practitioners and propitious circumstances. Additionally it was not concerned with the divine but could ascribe power to any object. Those who acquired the hair and nail parings of their enemies demonstrated the use of magic as an expression of hostility. These were submitted to some kind of abuse. The abuser hoped to gain power over his enemy. Freud suggests that this style of magic differed from sympathetic magic. The individual has tried to exert direct force through witchcraft. He has tried to supplant nature's laws with his own.

The individual played an important role in these proceedings because his belief in their power and importance formed the base from which they operated upon the culture. Their continuity in the life of the community depended upon the ability of the separate rites to hold the people together as a group and to satisfy their need for protection and economic security.

The use of body parts was equally distributed in these three rites of fertility, religion and magic although not always evenly within the same culture. It was only natural that one culture might have more reliance upon one particular factor than another culture. Hunting groups would not have been particularly concerned with the fertility rites of agricultural peoples. They would have used sympathetic magic to insure the increase of game. Some societies placed more emphasis upon magic than religion. To many American Indian tribes the shaman was more important that the priest because he dealt with the dark, illusory powers which the Indians sought out for guidance. The Ainu of Japan, on the other hand, denounced witchcraft as a dark art which was practiced in defiance of the will and spirit of the gods. In this instance the priest was more important than was the shaman. The desired end was to achieve a harmony with life and its vicissitudes through the use of these rites. The assurance of well being amidst a sea of conflicting and often frightening forces required sacrifice of the most extreme nature.

Where a total life was not given, as in human sacrifice, the next most important possession was rendered. That offering was a body part. There are numerous illustrations.

The notion of fertility has very often been associated with the shedding of blood. But the shedding of blood was not intended to take life away. Rather it was meant to give life. The blood was an offering to whatever being was supposed to benefit from its life energy. The god or animal was simply fed energy that it might be sustained. Often this bloodshed was allied with the practice of sympathetic magic.

The kangaroo hunt of the Arunta was preceded by bloodletting. This ceremony occurred near a grouping of rocks where the spirit of the Sacred Kangaroo was thought to dwell. At this point, where the sacred beast had entered the underworld, the young men opened their veins and let their blood flow over the rocks. As the kangaroo was a totem animal this act was perceived as recognition of the power of the totem and a good offering to give the totem power and strength. The desired result was an increase in the supply of kangaroo, the principal food for the Arunta.

Many hunting groups have used these blood rituals in the practice of sympathetic magic. A picture of the hunted animal is drawn on the ground. Blood from the hunters is smeared on that part of the picture that is considered to represent a vital organ. This wound is then transmitted to the actual animals in the process of hunting. The success of the hunt was thought to depend upon these rituals. The Kalahari bushmen performed this rite with such regularity and such great secrecy that the process took on the quality of a secret cult religion.

The practice of religion had its bloodshed rites as well. The Aztecs offered the blood and hearts of their victims to the gods. The Indians fed the mother goddess, Kali, with the blood of sacrificial victims. The horsemen of the steppe drank the blood of their enemies and gashed themselves at important religious functions. Bloodletting was a common practice because of the association of blood with life and life with the will and well being of the gods. The most devout were usually the most ready to propitiate the gods with their blood. In Malaysia there lived a group called the Semang. The Semang believed in a thunder god name Karei. Karei punished the violators of his taboos with thunderbolts. Thunder was thought to be a demonstration of Karei's anger. Those Semang who felt guilty would cut their shins, draw blood out and mix the blood with water. This mixture was made in a bamboo container that was then hurled at the thunder. The hope was to appease the god. Andre Malraux, in <u>La Voie Royale</u>, gives an interesting fictional account of some of the more barbaric practices of the peoples who lived in South East Asia.

The Aztecs practiced their own bloodletting ceremonies. They were a people who practiced self-punishment. Participants often cut themselves at public ceremonies as a demonstration of their piety. A hole was often cut in the tongue through which thorns were passed as a measure of atonement. During the great sacrificial rites, when thousands of slaves were put to death in honor of the sun god, the Aztec faithful gashed their ears and palms to be in union with the sacrifice. The priests, high in the political and social order, were the most ardent of these ritual bleeders.

The Indian devotees of the goddess Kali used other forms of self-torture. One form was called Yoga. The practitioners drove spits through the flesh, decorated their torsos with hooks that were set into the skin, and cut themselves with knives. They also lay for hours on beds of nails. These, and other practices, were a search for enlightenment and freedom from the desires of the flesh. Pain was the passage to the goddess.

Nowhere is the use of human parts more demonstrated than in the practice of the dark arts. As a simple amulet or an elaborate apparatus the tokens of esteem found their way into the practice of magic. This seems logical enough since any and all kinds of power and life were assigned to various parts of the body. The proper magical device assured protection against evil. The Vedas of Ceylon, an extremely primitive people, carried a piece of human liver in a pouch around the neck. In emergencies, such as confrontation with an enemy, the Veda would take this piece of flesh from the pouch and chew on it. This was supposed to give him super human strength allowing him to triumph over his enemy.

Prehistoric man knew the use of amulets. Human teeth were favorites in such decorations. In the La Comb Cave investigators discovered a human molar. The tooth had been drilled through and used as a pendant. An arrow was cut into the molar as a decoration. Any thought about the use of this tooth is conjecture but most probably it was an amulet and may have been a trophy of some kind.

Megalithic man used bones in his magic practices. In Western Europe archeologists have discovered numerous examples. Bones were converted into pendants or pipes. Skulls were discovered which had holes bored through them as though they were worn as a necklace. Some evidence of trepanation also exists suggesting a magical art. Maringer says that these skulls were operated upon after the owner was dead. See Johanes Maringer, The Gods of Prehistoric Man.

More modern peoples also believed in the magical properties of body parts. The Jivaro men of Ecuador sometimes wore a girdle made of human hair. This hair was taken from the head of one of their comrades who had died in battle. Only those who had demonstrated great courage in battle were honored in this manner. The hair was thought to transmit this courage to the wearer. The Cheyenne of the plains wore deerskin shirts in winter. These shirts were called war shirts because they were lined with the scalps of enemies. These scalps, taken in battle, were sewn on the seams of the shirt and were placed there to demonstrate the courage of the warrior.

Bones were sometimes used in primitive medical efforts. The Tasmanian shaman tried to induce supernatural powers in order to cure his patients. His principal tool was a rattle made from the bones of a dead man. The contemporary practice of Voodoo often makes use of the skull or bones of the dead to effect magical cures or even to bring sickness or disaster upon someone.

The Witoto of the Amazon used the bones of their victims for more practical endeavors. The long bones of the body were made into flutes. Some were also used as sticks to stir cooking pots. The head was set out for the ants to devour. When the head was picked clean the skull was placed on a pole in the village as a decoration. Human teeth were generally made into necklaces. The flesh was usually eaten.

Most of these practices represented the commonplace world of the people who indulged them. Their integrative value depended upon the degree to which these uses of the body were considered effective. A social acceptance of the power invested in human parts would logically enhance their effect upon community solidarity. A skull on top of a pole in the center of a village many not, in the long run, be much different than a flag.

Perhaps more important is the factor of impermanence. The use of special parts of the body was intended to ward off evil and death. To insure the regularity of life and the reliability of nature it was necessary, in the mind of the practitioner, to use some token of esteem. As a symbol of power that token had to come from the source of power and life, the human being.

## Rite de la Guerre

Self-esteem is one of the most poignant aspects of a warrior's life. Without some tangible measure of his worth a soldier is little more than an automaton, following orders. In the days when warfare was more personal combat and less mechanical destruction, the need for symbols of personal power was more immediate. In some societies the use of body parts as tokens of esteem became paramount to social recognition and military status. The warrior who could sport the most trophies was esteemed as the greatest warrior. A trophy taken, not from the personal possessions of an enemy, but from the enemy's body, was the greatest of triumphs.

The use of body parts as war tokens was not limited to the actual battles or wars. Sometimes rulers deprived unruly or disrespectful subjects of an ear, nose, eye or an entire head as a display of sovereign power. The story of Gatarzes, related at the start of this chapter, is a typical example. The Persian and Roman emperors were adept in the act of dismemberment. They indulged themselves for sport as often as for punishment or revenge. Nero went so far as to dip Christians in tar. These he would light and use as torches in the halls of his palaces.

Many of the examples, which will be included in this section, would fit as well in another. For the subjects of this discussion war was very often the apotheosis of all cultural life. Social events of importance were often dwarfed by the attention paid to war. Religion, fertility, magic and the rites of birth and passage were sometimes included in war. At least some portions of these rituals were connected to the military art. It is with this thought in mind that the following examples are presented.

The Indians of North America, above the Rio Grande, are usually associated with scalp hunting, a practice that they learned from the white man. The Pueblo Indians of the Southwest exercised an elaborate ritual in which the scalp represented the enemy who had been killed in battle. The scalp was much more than a simple trophy. This scalp dance was part of an initiation ceremony in which a young Zuni was admitted into the warrior cult. The scalp was offered homage through the recitation of special incantations, the purpose of which was to convert the scalp into one of the Zuni fetishes.

The principal concern of the Zuni was adequate rainfall. All of their deities were rain gods. The scalp was a prize, captured from another people, to which the Zuni prayed for rain. The scalp, in some manner, became the protector of the Zuni. Compare this with the practice of the Celts who put the heads of their enemies above the doorway to protect their houses from evil. The person who took the scalp became a person of importance because of his "addition" to the sum total of tribal welfare. These scalps were preserved in the scalp house where they became the responsibility of the war chiefs and the warrior cult.

The Eastern regions of the United States had tribes of Indians that did not limit their war trophies to scalps. Their wars were not restricted either. The Iroquois were at war with every tribe with which they did not have an alliance. The typical trophy was the scalp. This was removed from the victim, stretched and fire dried. Sometimes the entire head was taken. The Iroquois tortured their captives until they died. Fingers were bitten off. The torso was roasted over a fire. Sometimes Iroquois warriors ate the body for its strength and virtue. In some instances the heart alone was consumed. The object of all this was the object of war in general, to win glory and prestige. Rather than a political venture, war was an individual enterprise. Anyone with the approval of the tribe could make war.

There were other, more gruesome, practices in which body parts were used as an expression of personal power or religious fervor. We have stated that the Aztec culture was a civilization dominated by warriors. The principal activity of war was to find victims to sacrifice. Most of these sacrifices were centered on the use of the heart. Stone boxes for the storage and the burning of human hearts were constructed by the Aztecs out of lava and decorated with images depicting the gods to whom these sacrifices were made. One such box was the Great Sacrifice Stone mentioned in chapter two. The container was eight feet in diameter and two and one half feet thick. Many a heart was dislodged from war captives to be burned ceremoniously in this great stone.

Another people of Meso-America, the Tarascans, tore the hearts of their victims out and threw them into sacred springs. This ceremony was called the Rain Dance. These were hot springs and the hearts were thrown in to "feed" the spring. The rising steam from these waters was believed to turn into rain clouds at the instigation of the rain god.

Flayed skin was a common item of use among the Aztecs. The Aztec god, Xipe, represented springtime and the vegetation which covers the earth in springtime. War captives were often flayed. The priests used their skins as cloaks. This practice was in honor of Xipe. The skin was symbolic of the vegetative covering. The skin of the corn maiden was used in the same way. One rite, concerned with the healing powers of the god, used human skin as a curative medium. The sick person donned this article in the hope of being healed by its putative power.

The white man had his share of these activities as well although his participation was not always a ritual. In the 19th century, in the Western United States, a band of Cheyenne warriors was defeated in battle. They surrendered to a unit of American soldiers near Denver, Colorado. The battle was called Sand Hills, not to be confused with the more infamous Sand Creek. The Indians were all shot to death. Their arms and legs were cut off as trophies. Later, these appendages were displayed in a Denver theater for the amusement and to the applause of the white "citizens."

The Vikings practiced a different kind of torture, which, according to Gwyn Jones, had a religious meaning. The rite was called "carving the blood eagle on the back." The victim was stretched out on his stomach. An incision was made along the length of his spinal column. The ribs were pulled away from his spinal column and his lungs were pulled out and spread across his back as though they were wings. This was an extremely painful way to die.

Demonstrating sexual prowess was another aspect of the warrior's trophy search. The warrior made a connection between his own self-image and his potency or virility. In some cases the tribe member went into battle, killed the enemy and amputated the genital organs of the enemy. This part of the foe's anatomy was then worn on the warrior's belt. The wearing of this ornament was believed to augment the warrior's courage and sense of manhood.

One might expect that this kind of practice would be limited to extremely isolated ethnocentric groups. The facts reveal that more civilized peoples have indulged themselves in similar practices. An incident occurred at the Sand Creek Massacre in which the Nez Perce women and children were mutilated. Their private parts were cut out. One woman had been repeatedly raped. Then her persecutors cut out her genital parts. The soldier who took this "trophy" placed it upon a stick and ran about waving the stick as though it were a flag or a souvenir. For a graphic account of this incident see Susan Brownmiller, <u>Against Our Will, Men Women and Rape</u>.

Not surprisingly blood was a favorite tool of the soldier. Herodotus says that the Greeks swore oaths on each other's blood. The two parties to the oath cut one of their arms. Then each man licked the other's blood to seal the bond. The Scythians had a more elaborate practice. The two oath takers cut themselves and allowed their blood to flow into an earthenware vessel. This jar was filled with wine. Prayers were said. Swords, spears and arrows were dipped into the mixture. The oath was sworn. Then the warriors, the chief and the most important followers of the chief drank the concoction to seal the oath.

In his history of Lysander, the historian Plutarch recounts a story about the Athenians during the siege of their city in 405 BC. At the insistence of their generals they passed a decree requiring that all prisoners of war were to be mutilated. Their right thumbs were amputated. The purpose of this rather brutal surgery was to insure that the prisoners could not throw spears, a principal weapon of the time. This would not prevent them from rowing with oars in the Athenian ships. However efficient this practice was to the military mind it reflects a kind of insensitivity and cruelty, which was common in the Near East and beyond. See Plutarch, <u>The Rise and Fall of Athens</u>.

The Eastern monarchs, especially the Persian and Assyrian emperors, were adept at this art. The ritual became known as a cultural specialty among these tyrants. Ashurnasirpal II, a king of Assyria, made this cruelty a standard policy. When his men conquered a people, the unfortunate victims lost their arms and feet. They were piled into a heap as the king could watched their owners suffocate to death. The Mongol conqueror, Ghengis Khan, beheaded the inhabitants of the lands he overwhelmed. In this manner he could count the number of those who had been defeated. These heads were stacked in piles.

The Persians were the most infamous of the lot. Cambyses, a Persian king, once punished a royal judge by having him flayed. The skin of the victim was torn from his body and cut into strips. These strips of flesh were used to line the back of the king's chair. The king then reminded newly appointed judges of the material of which his throne was made. They must not forget their duty. The lesson of the king's power over his subjects was not lost upon them. See Herodotus, The Histories.

This same Persian King Cambyses launched an invasion against Egypt. His armies were under the command of a Greek mercenary named Phanes. It seems that Phanes had once been in the employ of the Egyptians. There was great enmity between the two sides. Some of the Greek mercenaries who were fighting for the Egyptians captured two of the sons of Phanes. The victims were brought out in front of the two armies. Their throats were slit, the blood from their necks dripping into a cauldron. Then all of the Greek mercenaries on the Egyptian side drank the blood in full view of Phanes. Despite this, Phanes won the battle.

The integration of the warrior into his cult relied on his ability to find a rank in the social order that was befitting to his prowess and his accomplishments. The ranks shifted with the changing fortunes of war. Men were killed or wounded. Others took their place in the ranks. The principal mark of the warrior was the trophy he took in battle, a trophy that gave rise to the kinds of examples discussed above.

The cultural selection of inhumanity in these cases rested upon the emphasis that the warrior placed upon his status. The selection seems to have rested upon the desire of the individual warrior to gain prestige at some other's expense. Emasculation of an enemy was a common manner of demonstrating that power. Head hunting was even more popular. The concern about courage was expressed in bloodletting rites and self-torture. The mutilation of subjects by rulers is typical of the need to have some physical evidence for one's authority, some tangible token of esteem, for all to see.

Rite de la Mort

The last social and cultural enterprise of an individual is his death and burial. Such occasions bring together people who are linked by ties of friendship and kinship. This community closes ranks to send the departed on to another world. The manner in which this send off is accomplished depends upon the communal perception of that other world. The question about death, which is most emphatically answered by culture, defines the relationship between the hereafter and the here and now. Does the individual journey to a new and separate existence where his ties with his former life are severed or does he maintain some spiritual contact with the living?

Many people have accepted this concept of an underworld to which the dead travel, were supposed to travel and where they were supposed to dwell, at least for a period of time. Russell says that the underworld has been an ambivalent conception for many peoples, representing both good and evil. A place of darkness and cold on the one hand, it also represented fertility and the cycles of nature on the other. Things are born, they die and they are reborn. For that reason death has often been associated with sexuality. Most peoples have shunned death as a terrible finality while at the same time accepting death as an ineluctable and necessary part of living. See Jeffrey Burton Russell, <u>The Devil. Perceptions of Evil from Earliest times to Primitive Christianity</u>.

The use of body parts was, and to some degree still is, an important part of this last social act of the individual. We shall consider these uses in five specific categories. First there was the expression of mourning which inspired a certain amount of self-torture or dismemberment. There was some attempt to preserve parts of the deceased as mementos. Relics are a typical use of the body; a practice still used by Catholics and Buddhists. Third, there was an attempt to keep some of the qualities of the deceased, especially for magical uses. A fourth instance was the deliberate dishonoring of an individual who had escaped, through death, some kind of punishment. Desecration was a common example of revenge. Finally, for those who believed that the spirit of the dead might be harmful to the living, there were deliberate attempts to prevent the dead from returning. Scattering the remains of the deceased was a usual practice. Prehistoric man buried his dead under large stones or bound the body tightly in a flexed position to achieve the same end. Some examples will demonstrate how these attitudes were put into practice to deal with the problem of impermanence.

The mortal loss of a tribal member was final. Death inspired a variety of sympathetic acts designed to demonstrate the feelings of remorse and loss. Persons close to the deceased would literally give something of themselves at the funeral. A common offering was accomplished by severing a joint of the finger. This was an expression of mourning as well as an attempt to stop other deaths among the tribal group. The Dugum Dani of New Guinea practiced this rite whenever a tribesman died in battle. They selected a young girl from among his family members. Her finger joint was amputated. A series of wars or epidemics could leave a woman's hand with nothing but stubs. This act was believed to placate the ghost of the dead man. Maijno described the same practice among the Kalahari bushmen and the Indians of Northwestern Canada. Cheyenne females who were related to a warrior killed in battle sometimes cut off a finger joint. Clansmen of a deceased Crow Indian did the same. See Guido Maijno, The Healing Hand, Man and Wound in the Ancient World.

Chapter two included a description of a Scythian king's funeral in which mourners cut their ears, gashed their arms and legs and jabbed arrows into their hands. These practices were customary among the people of the Eurasian steppes and are still practiced in some areas. The Western Plains Indians of the United States were no different. The Cheyenne woman wailed and moaned while cutting her arms and legs and generating a general feeling of despair. Burial rites for a Crow Indian included the participation of clansmen in a funeral procession. These mourners cut strips of flesh from their arms and legs. In addition, they lacerated their scalps so that blood would flow freely over their entire bodies. The peoples of Meso-America, such as the Aztecs, let blood flow for any reason, especially a funeral.

Hair was another item frequently forfeited in death rituals. The shaving of the dead Arunta to make a hair belt for his oldest son has already been discussed in this chapter. The belt was never given to the younger son. Female relatives of the Cheyenne cut off all of their hair as a sign of mourning. The Crow Indians did not. The men valued their hair very much and were willing to part with only a very small lock of hair for the deceased. Herodotus described the practice among the Hyperboreans and the Scythians. Both males and females cut their hair as a sign of mourning as did the Greeks.

Hair cutting, finger joint amputation and bloodletting were physical manifestations of inner feelings and not just a culturally acceptable expression. These practices represented something else. They confined death and its mourning to a ritual and public act. By offering these parts of the anatomy the mourners said farewell to the deceased and then put him or her out of mind. In some societies the name could never again be spoken. The mourners had allowed a small part of themselves to die in commiseration of the departed. Thus the subject of death could be closed. The payment had been made.

The preservation of the remains of the dead went hand in hand with the attempt to preserve some of his virtues. Although life had departed from him, certain vital characteristics remained. These qualities were thought to be of benefit to his survivors. Those societies that adhered strongly to the belief in magic attached great importance to such tokens. Such was the attitude of the Yukagir of Siberia toward their shaman. The shamans were thought to be extremely powerful even after they were dead. Some believed that shamans could actually leave their bodies and travel into the dark world in the body of another human or that of an animal. Great care was thus taken in the disposition of the shaman's body. Otherwise he might return, find his body abused and wreak havoc upon the people of his village. The flesh of the shaman was cut into strips, each strip being worn as an amulet for power and protection. The bones of the sorcerer were dressed and placed in a special location in the home. His children venerated his bones. Other shamans consulted the bones on special occasions concerning important tribal matters such as hunting. Hunting was the principal economic activity of the tribe.

Chapter one described a similar practice among the Manu of Melanesia who preserved the skull of their patriarch in a shrine where the family of the chief could venerate his spirit. The Tahitian chiefs were also preserved. The body was eviscerated, the brain was removed, and the skin was baked in the sunshine so that it would dry. The corpse was then buried without the skull. After the scalp had decomposed the skull was taken to the Marae, the sacred ground of Tahiti where it was properly venerated.

The people of the Cauca Valley in South America indulged in a more elaborate version of this custom. Warriors that had been captured in battle were dutifully sacrificed to the gods. Through a process of fire drying and the application of wax and ashes these bodies were preserved. They were outfitted with military clothing and weapons and housed in a special museum where they remained on display as a testimony to the power of their captors. Their strength was thought to reside within their bodies. These bodies were supposed to become the servants of the captors when the captors also died. These peoples also preserved the bodies of their greatest war chiefs, using the same methods. The mummies of the chiefs were carried into battle as a source of inspiration for the common soldiers.

There were other, less complete, uses of the body. When a Trobriand Islander died his corpse became a source of relics. Many bones were removed and used in a very practical manner. The husband's skull became the wife's lime pot. His jawbone was worn on a string as a necklace. Edmund Spencer reported a similar ritual among the Andaman Islanders who strung the small bones of their dead to make necklaces. These necklaces were given as gifts. Their putative magical powers could prevent or cure disease. The Trobrianders had no fear of their dead and disposed of the remains freely. The Andamaners feared the flesh of the deceased. They waited until the corpse had decayed before collecting the magic bones. The Arunta of Australia had the same profound belief in magic and magical charms. They believed that sorcery was the cause of disease and death. The previously mentioned belt of human hair taken from the dead man was considered to be a very powerful charm. See Elman Service, <u>A Profile of Primitive Culture</u>.

The Tasmanians believed that some ghosts were benevolent. These specters included the spirits of departed relatives. The bones of their kinsmen were collected from the pile that remained after cremation. These were worn as amulets and gave the wearer protection from malevolent ghosts. The widow, or another close relative, often wore the skull of the deceased for protection. This apparel was also a sign of mourning. When the wife of a Polynesian Dobu died, her body was buried intact. Some time later the skull was unearthed and used in a ritual dance performed by the children of the paternal aunt. This was a kind of farewell ceremony for the spirit. The skull was preserved and given to a cousin as a keepsake.

Some African peoples made such preservations also. The skull of the Ganda king was separated from his body six months after his death. One man was designated to drink a mixture of milk and beer from the king's skull He thus became the official medium through which the dead king spoke to his people. The king's jawbone was placed in a special shrine. The skull was sealed with the king's body in his tomb.

These relics of the dead were very popular in many areas of the world. The multitude of Buddhist reliquaries in the eastern world provided thrill seekers and devotees of the Enlightened One an opportunity to touch some magical bones. Perhaps the relic was represented as the tooth of the Buddha or that of one of his saints. Entire skeletons were picked apart in order to distribute relics among the faithful. These practices continue to the present day among Buddhists. Catholics preserve the bones of their saints as well. Official relics even have a certificate of authenticity. Altars in Catholic churches may contain one or more of these bones. In a sense these relics link the physical and temporal community to the spiritual community. They did the same for ethnocentric peoples.

Death also engendered a sense of fear agitated by a feeling of confronting something inexplicable and uncontrolled. Efforts were made to keep the dead from coming back as though they might make trouble for the living. Sometimes the possessions of the deceased were broken. Often the body was tied or weighted with heavy stones. Other groups practiced cremation. More extreme cases involved cannibalism. The name of the dead man was barred from use. His house was destroyed. On occasion the entire village was abandoned.

The logic behind all of this is perhaps best expressed by the example of the Arunta. The nearest relative of the deceased smashed the skull to pieces. The arms and legs were broken. This practice aimed at keeping the ghost from chasing anyone or from haunting the mind. The motivation may have lacked validity but the fear was real. The deceased must be mollified. Such practices may have been considered necessary because the dead man had been deprived of life, the most valuable of his possessions. His spirit might be resentful about the loss. See Ruth Benedict, Patterns of Culture.

The final consideration in this section is the deliberate desecration of the body for the purpose of revenge, punishment or the release of personal hostility. Earlier we recounted a story from Plutarch about Megacles whose followers had been caught cheating another group. Those who were living had been found guilty by the Athenians and fined. Those who had died were treated differently. Their bodies were dug up and thrown over the border of the kingdom. This practice of desecrating bodies or simply throwing them out to public spectacle was quite common. Criminals were hung out for display. The Persian king Xerxes once had a man split in two parts. Each of these halves was used as a road marker. The victim had offended the king. The Persian army marched past these markers and marked the lesson well! Plutarch recounts another such tale in his history of Nicias. Two Athenian generals, who had been accused of wrong doing, killed themselves to avoid punishment. The Athenians threw their bodies outside the city gate for a public spectacle. See Plutarch, <u>The Rise and Fall of Athens.</u>

This desecration had a religious theme for some. The biblical king Josiah, in his attempt to lead the Hebrews away from the worship of Baal and the practice of human sacrifice, destroyed many of the heathen temples. In one place of sacrifice he discovered a number of tombs dedicated to the cult of Baal. These he opened so that his men might burn the bones on the altar in defilement of the cult.

The Tasmanians had a fervor for desecration. When an enemy was killed in battle his body was hauled to the village. All adult males joined in hacking the body to bits until virtually nothing recognizable remained. The Tasmanians had not achieved even the rudiments of agriculture so the practice cannot be perceived as a fertility rite. The unfortunate victim was simply the focal point of an intense outburst of aggression.

The use of body parts in death rituals clearly reflects the integrative functions of both religion and magic. A single item brought the group to focus upon a single and important aspect of life. The emotional response to death was reinforced by the personal and collective attachment to some memento of the deceased. The personal sacrifice of one's body parts intensified that emotion and the commitment to the norms and expectations of the group. A few drops of blood, an old sun whitened skull or an amputated finger joint provided the community with a means to effect the holistic expression of its existence and purpose.

In death the confrontation with the problem of impermanence is unavoidable. The attempt to preserve mementos and to ascribe to those keepsakes magical or supernatural powers was clearly an effort to thwart the idea of finality. The idea that the community could derive some lasting benefit from the parting of one of its members is a clear attempt to confront the prospect of change. Even the attempt to dissuade the return of the dead recognized death as another kind of existence. These rituals and their tokens were also helpful in instructing each new generation about community attitudes toward death.

The Question of Esteem

There can be no question that the body parts described in this chapter were tokens of esteem. Each community found some way to use these tokens as a badge of honor or recognition. Whether the token was taken from an enemy or a friend, from a tribesman or a kinsman, the intention was a demonstration of power over the environment. The physical symbol of what was once alive and functioning, however gruesome to behold, was a mark of self assurance and autonomy in a world plagued by uncertainty. The tiniest portions of man were the greatest of his tokens of esteem.

# 5

## *A Necklace for Kali*

Kali was the Hindu goddess of death. She was the earth mother, the timeless deity, who recycled life and death. Her skin was dark and cold like the hollow of the earth. Her taste ran to human flesh and her appetite was voracious. Many an unwitting victim was "fed" to Kali. Her body was covered with garments made from the bones of those who were her sustenance. Their heads were strung to make her necklace, a necklace for Kali. It was said that one properly sacrificed victim could feed the goddess for a thousand years.

Her temples were filled with many and gruesome horrors, among them the screams of those who were sacrificed. Drains were built into her altars to allow the rich, red blood to flow into the bosom of the mother earth. Heartless executioners with grim faces and razor sharp knives attended their duties to the goddess with speed and precision. The head of each new victim was proffered to the goddess after having been displayed to the throng of devoted worshipers, those who were witnesses to the deed. Black and cruel was this goddess, this Kali, this porter of death whose very whim meant the lives of countless devotees, whose necklace was ever being strung with fresh beads.

This chapter is about headhunters and cannibals. Ordinarily one might think of headhunters and cannibals as being very primitive and isolated peoples. In many instances that supposition is quite correct. Even the technology of the twentieth century has failed to proscribe all of them. In the darkest parts of several continents the practice continues unabated. But we are concerned with much more than the tribal practices of remote areas such as the Solomon Islands or the Amazon Basin. These crafts were practiced among civilized peoples with much the same motivations as their less developed neighbors. Although the practice was very specialized and regulated by extremely precise ritual the outcome was the same, the decapitation and consumption of human beings!

For the purposes of our discussion head hunting will be considered in three categories. They are the act of warfare, the demonstration of power and the function of religion and death. There are other categories in which these practices might be placed but these are the ordinary instances of the art. As this is not a discussion of the history of criminal justice, the treatment of decapitation as a capital punishment will be peripheral. One should note that such punishment continues in some areas of the Middle East where certain crimes are punished by this method. Some general comments about head hunting are in order.

Among preliterate peoples head hunting was often a social requirement for a variety of cultural activities such as marriage, funerals and entrance into the adult world. At least these were the requirements for the male. These rites were not peripheral but integral to the continuity of the social structure. In Borneo, the entire tribal structure depended upon head hunting as a cohesive bond. When colonial authorities discouraged head hunting, there was a concomitant breakdown in the tribal culture. The same phenomenon was reported in the Solomon Islands. Restrictions on the practice of head hunting resulted in the rapid and complete dissolution of the social compact.

Chapter four discussed a number of ways in which parts of the body were used ritually. Practitioners paid more attention to the head than to any other body part. Even among civilized peoples, the head seems to have been the grandest trophy of all. One made a concerted effort to display heads as trophies. At the end of a battle heads were piled up or used as necklaces, drinking cups and guardians of sacred places. The Aztecs kept a head rack upon which all of the heads taken during human sacrifice were displayed. The Thracians put the heads of their enemies on the points of their spears and then paraded around wildly. The Tinguians of Indonesia kept a "head" tree. The Celts placed heads on the poles above their chimneys to ward off evil spirits. Some warrior cults, such as the Celts, wore heads on their belts as ornaments. We have already mentioned the disposition of heads by the devotees of the goddess Kali.

In Europe this affection for skulls reached into prehistoric times. In the Gutari Cave a skull was discovered in the center of a ring of stones. No other parts of the body were evident. The Foramen Magnum had been enlarged. This is the large aperture in the base of the skull through which the brain is connected to the spinal cord. This is evidence of deliberate brain extraction that may be an example of brain cannibalism or a two-stage burial. Some peoples were afraid of the flesh of corpses. They allowed the flesh to rot before they buried the bones. The brain, being encased in the skull, decays more slowly. The extraction of the brain through the foramen magnum would facilitate burial of the skull. The skull belonged to a male. There was a large dent in the right temple area suggesting that the owner had died by violence. Maringer suggested that the treatment of this skull indicated the possibility of a skull cult, which relied upon magic. See Johannes Maringer, The Gods of Prehistoric Man.

A more emphatic example is the group of prehistoric caves at Ofnet in Germany. Excavators found two nests of skulls, a total of twenty-two, arranged in two concentric circles. The marks on the skulls suggest that all were decapitated. Breuil says that this was done with a flint knife. Most of the skulls also showed evidence of having been struck with a blunt instrument. This evidence implies that the twenty-two men, women and children had been massacred. The skulls were laid in a bed of ocher and were covered with red ocher. Most skulls were those of women and children. These were decorated with shells and teeth. The skulls of the men were not decorated. Investigators dated these skulls from the Neolithic period and believed that they were part of a head hunting and cannibal ritual. See Henri Breuil, <u>The Men of the Old Stone Age</u>.

There must have been considerable preoccupation with skulls in the early Neolithic. Most of the remains of Ice Age Europe support this idea. While there have been a number of skeletons discovered intact, most of the findings are limited to the skull or the skull cap as though these people possessed a preference for heads at the expense of the rest of the body. The later peoples, such as the Celts and the Vikings, generally held to this same preference. This is not conclusive evidence but the data does support the idea that the trend in head hunting and brain cannibalism was very ancient in Europe.

The emphasis upon the head is well established. The question of why is more elusive a matter. Why should so much attention be paid to the head? One reason is that the head was representative of the deceased. His facial features separated him from all the others of his kind and made of him an individual. The preservation of the face was important in funeral rites, as the visage was a keepsake for the mourners. The Egyptians went to great efforts to preserve the facial features of the pharaoh by making a mask of gold in his likeness. In war the same concept was applied in identifying the enemy who had been killed or the rival who had been vanquished. The king, having ordered the death of a subject located in a distant part of the kingdom, could have the victim's head as proof of his death. The truly paranoid tyrant gained some self-assurance by being able to look at the heads of his supposed enemies.

Secondly, the head was a symbol of power. Chapter four discussed the uses of the head in magic rites. These included the use of heads as amulets. The veneration of skulls of ancestors was also important. In terms of power, the display of heads was often more important than the taking of heads. The displayed head was a sign of the victor's power over his enemies. Whether that victor was an Aztec priest, a Persian emperor or a Celtic or Thracian warrior, the purpose was the same, a demonstration of power. One need only recall the story of Herod, Salome and John the Baptist.

To ancient peoples, the head was as vital an organ as it is to we modern peoples. All the senses of the body, which register environmental parameters, are in the head. Sight, smell, hearing and taste in many of these peoples, living in a hostile and primitive environment, were much more sensitive and important than that of our own. The head is the repository of memory and the "think tank" of the body. It is also the instrument of verbal and facial communication. The expression of emotion in a culture with few words relies heavily upon appearance. Our subjects recognized these attributes of the head and reasoned that all vital processes could be halted, and possibly preserved, if the head were removed and kept.

Head hunting has also been explained as a demonstration of sexual prowess. Freudian implications aside, this idea makes sense if sexual power is defined in terms of overall physical and mental vitality. Head taking would then be a reflection of one's physical and mental agility. Many warrior cults placed a high value on these qualities, especially in their leaders. It should be no surprise that head hunting was often a qualification for adult status and recognition. The Scythians held a provincial meeting at the end of each year in which the governor of the province served wine to all adult warriors. Those who had not taken a head in battle were excluded from this ceremony and put to shame by that very exclusion. Among the Sarmatians, who were related to the Scythians, a standing rule required that no woman could be married until she had taken a head in battle. This is the source of the Greek stories about the legendary Amazon warriors. To the extent that war, power and religion determined the ordinary processes of cultural development and the place of individuals in the pecking order, heads were first among the tokens of esteem.

The second part of this chapter will consider cannibalism, defined as the consumption of some part of the body. There are a number of misconceptions about cannibals that cloud the issue and significance of the practice. One misconception is that all cannibals were very primitive peoples. While it is true that many technically unsophisticated and ecologically isolated peoples engaged in cannibalism, there were other, more advance, peoples, such as the Persians and the Aztecs, who indulged in these practices. We have mentioned several cultures whose technology included the use of iron and the manufacture of artwork from precious metals. They were fond of drinking the blood of their enemies. Celts, Scythians and Thracians were certainly above the level of primitive savages. Technological and social sophistication do not preclude and are not mutually exclusive of the cannibal act.

Another misconception is that all primitives are or were cannibals. This idea dates from the early European explorations. The sixteenth century European perception of African peoples included a belief that cannibalism was widespread and frequent among the natives that, allegedly, spared neither friend nor foe. Their craving for human flesh was said to be beyond all limits. Katherine George in her <u>Study in Ethnocentrism 1400-1800</u> maintained that cannibalism was not widespread in Africa and was restricted to certain ceremonial functions. She admits that there may have been isolated occurrences of non-ceremonial cannibalism but not on the scale suggested by 16th century explorers. In an address to the Council of the Indies in 1525 the Spaniard Ortiz accused the Indians of eating human flesh.

Pierre Vidal-Naquet, in his book, <u>Les Assassins de la Mémoire</u>, quotes the Spanish explorer Bernal Diaz del Castillo. "Pour ce qui est de manger de la chair humaine, on peut dire qu'ils en faisant usage absolument comme nous de la viande de boucherie." This was, however, an attempt to cover up the atrocities of the forced labor systems imposed by the Spanish on the Indians. For an excellent account of the attitudes toward indigenous peoples in the Americas see, Eduardo Galeano, <u>Las Venas Abiertas de America Latina</u>. The fact is that very few peoples have practiced cannibalism as a consistent or large-scale enterprise.

The most popular myth is that cannibalism was an effort to supplement a vegetable diet with animal protein in the absence of game. There is a half-truth in this argument. In the rain forests of Africa and the island of Polynesia some peoples supplemented their diets with human flesh. Their reaction to the absence of animal protein was the same as any human being that might be confronted with a serious absence of food. They ate human flesh to survive. The Donner Pass Party in the American West in the 19th century ate some of their fellow passengers in order to make it through the winter. Some years ago there was a plane crash in the Andes in which the survivors ate the flesh of their dead comrades in order to sustain themselves. There are other examples that reflect the basic impulse for survival under adverse conditions, a fact characteristic of human beings. These examples are representative of extreme need and do not reflect a cultural bias or disposition to anthropophagy.

The fact is that cannibalism was a highly developed ritual that recognized magical properties in human flesh and blood. These properties could be preserved and imbued by consuming human parts. This attitude reflects a very close attachment to the cycles of nature. This attitude reflects an understanding of how nature controls the ebb and flow of life. Those societies that have had the greatest affinity to cannibalism have recognized that man is an integral part of the rest of existence and does not lose his spiritual properties by death. They are simply transformed. The societies which have had the greatest abhorrence of cannibalism are those which place a high premium on the separation of man and nature. The belief in the resurrection of the body in a spiritual way precludes the act of cannibalism. These differences have usually been divided along the lines of east and west with primitive cultures being defined as backward and degenerate. The facts suggest a difference in perception rather than the absence of ethical or moral behavior.

As cannibalism was an attempt to preserve the qualities of human beings the question becomes one of what qualities and whose body. Both endocannibalism and exocannibalism were practiced with this view in mind. The slash and burn agrarian cultures of South East Asia were known to kill and eat their old people so that the strength and wisdom of the tribe would not be lost to the community. This endocannibalism was designed to strengthen the overall communal ties that enhanced the survival of what was always a group balanced on the thin line of survival. The Tinguians of Indonesia practiced brain cannibalism in conjunction with their head hunting ventures. Young girls prepared the brain of the dead enemy, a symbol of fertility, and fed the brain to the warriors, a verification of libidinal prowess. Ritual was designed to accommodate circumstance to perception and need.

Anthropophagy reflected the art of warfare, the demonstration of power and the need for religion. Similar to other uses of body parts, the act of cannibalism was an effort to derive some spiritual benefit from a physical, human object. The value of the practice was in its ability to provide the participant with a sense of security, a feeling of solidarity with his group. The rite gave him an assurance that his action preserved the net balance of all human virtue.

These practices were widespread. The evidence hints at the idea that these rites may have been part of an evolutionary process in which culture developed from a terrestrial to a celestial view of life. We have already mentioned these lines in the discussion of eastern and western culture. The argument may be false and irrelevant but it does suggest a basis for cultural development that does not insist upon a relationship between humanity and a linear technological advance. The Nazis obviously discredited that contention. These practices were cultural options rather than developmental phases.

The following sections of this chapter will try to demonstrate the integrative value of head hunting and cannibalism in the practices of human culture. The hope of the human spirit in its ability to control the destiny of man and his environment will become evident in the insistent belief in the power of the human body even long after it has failed to demonstrate any sign of life or purpose. Like their modern counterparts, the headhunters and cannibals of past times were reaching out for the eternal.

## The Art of War

Head hunting was often a requirement for full social recognition. The acquisition and display of heads was a mark of warrior status. This status may have been restricted to entry into the warrior cult or it may have been an avenue for social and political advancement. The opportunities depended upon the emphasis that was placed upon head hunting by the community. Social situations and tensions predicated upon clan membership and primogeniture were often alleviated by the ceremonies connected to this practice. Younger sons, who would otherwise have been deprived of social recognition, could win a suitable place for themselves by the exposition of their martial skills.

Kalinga warriors earned prestige by hunting heads. Social status was usually determined through birth but an adept headhunter could rise above his station. Noteworthy persons were given a particular and distinctive tattoo separating them from ordinary folks. Their words carried more weight in the community council. At the conclusion of head hunting rituals younger sons of the tribe, those who had been victimized by the laws of primogeniture, were sometimes given grants of land. As with the Aztecs, property was a measure of Kalinga wealth. Land was a reward for the faithful and efficient execution of public duty.

The headhunting raids were sporadic. Blood vengeance disputes, some of which were passed from generation to generation, were the cause and justification of the raid. Raiders entered the enemy territory by stealth. A passerby was captured and killed. His head was taken back to the village where the trophy was placed on a stake in the center of the village. The warriors held a dance around the head and, in the process, extracted the brain. This tissue they mixed with sugar cane juice and then consumed.

In Ecuador, each male Jivaro was expected to be a warrior by profession. The chief claim to prestige was the number of heads that a warrior had taken in battle. The targets for this quest, unlike those of the Kalinga, were specific. That is to say that victims were not chosen by reason of blood vengeance. The typical victim was a male of another tribe. Old people, regardless of their sex, were also targets. Women and children were taken captive for their obvious utility. The warriors returned to the village with these trophies for a victory celebration in which each successful raider was allowed to recount his exploits in the battle.

Before these trophies could become proper symbols of warrior status they must be processed. The skin was peeled from the skull and boiled. The boiling reduced the scalp to one third of its original size. Hot stones were placed inside the scalp to dry the skin and reduce the size even more. Hot sand was also used for this purpose. The head was smoked over the fire for a number of hours. This helped to preserve the finished product that the Jivaro called a Tsantsas. This properly prepared trophy was then used to call attention to the warrior and his greatness. Tsantsas had other, religious and social functions. The Jivaro enterprise seems to have been more a collective and socially oriented effort than that of the Kalinga. Personal aggrandizement or revenge was discarded in favor of the needs of the community.

The Samoan hunter, like the Jivaro, considered his proudest achievement in war to be the taking of an enemy head. These prizes were returned to the village and displayed before the chief. Each head was added to a pile of heads, stacked in the shape of a pyramid. The position of any war trophy in the pyramid was in direct relationship to the status of the individual warrior who had secured it and the status of the warrior whose head it had been. The victim of highest rank among the enemy was the one whose head was at the top of the pile. The Samoans placed more emphasis upon collective display of trophies than upon individual achievement.

The motivation for war among the Samoans was somewhat different due to the island nature of their existence. The geographic arrangement of tribes created fringe elements in two competing neighborhoods. These border elements were the ones who initiated most warrior actions. Thus all Samoans were not headhunters. Murdock suggested that this situation made head hunting more or less a specialization of war. This may also have helped to provide minor victories which would be experienced by both sides in sufficient numbers to preclude a major outbreak of hostilities or the need for a general mobilization of warriors to counter every enemy threat. In other words they engaged in limited border wars. The burden of personal security was placed upon the wariness of the individual instead of upon the resources of the state. The specialization of tasks in warfare also provided "heroes" whose exploits stood out from those of the ordinary soldier.

The Celts placed great value upon heads as a sign of their prowess. Chapter one describes their practice of wearing such ornaments on their belts. The use of skulls as drinking cups was also popular, especially among the leaders who brought out their favorite skulls to show off before visiting dignitaries. The richer and more powerful a man was the more attention was paid to the decoration of the skull. A poor warrior might line his skull with leather but the mighty and affluent chieftain, whose reputation might be at stake, had nothing but a gold lining. Diodorus Siculus said that the heads of the most important victims were placed in oil and stored in wooden boxes that they might be preserved and attest to the valor of the victor.

The head as a status symbol was very important to the Celts, more important than victory. Livy says that the Celts, who were once besiegers of Rome, failed to follow up on their imminent victory over the city because they did not immediately enter Rome. The reason, he says, was their need to cut off the heads of those who had fallen in battle. Heads were so important that they were nailed to the doors of houses and on the trunks of trees in the sacred groves. Heads were a measure of a warrior's power over his enemies.

To the Celts the terrible spectacle of a decapitated head was more than a trophy of war. The head was a focal point for the history of war. The head was used as a conversational piece, an opening gambit in any discussion of past battles. The warrior would demonstrate to his listeners how the head had been taken, perhaps pointing to the sword or knife with which the deed had been done. His account would include an assessment of the enemy, his strength and skill, the difficulty encountered in defeating him. All of this was designed to increase his status in the warrior cult.

The capture and display of human heads seems to have involved a good deal more than just warrior status. The reinforcement of the warrior's position was important but the affirmation of cultural inclinations and dispositions was imperative. Perhaps the display of heads suggests an acceptance of certain kinds of violence projected outward. This would insure harmony within. A kind of culturally sanctioned wildness may have been a release valve for community tensions. Dancing and chanting could provide a heightened cathartic release, if accompanied by some tokens of blood lust.

The Nootka Indians of British Columbia felt such an imperative. The Nootka were by nature a very peaceable tribe, not given to violence or savagery. However, they believed that warfare was equivalent to the complete annihilation of their enemies. With the element of surprise they attacked an enemy village and killed every inhabitant. All heads were taken, even those of the women and children. The trophies were placed upon spear points. Raids were followed by ceremonies including wild dancing and great pomp.

In terms of group dynamics the actions of the Nootka demonstrate a profoundly integrative pattern. The enemy, the object of a savage and irrational hatred and contempt, was external to the community. The process of what Konrad Lorenz has called subspeciation dispelled the ordinary tensions that existed within groups. That is the Nootka were able to identify themselves as a distinct and homogeneous race with a demonstrable superiority to their neighbors. As long as they were successful in war they effected communal solidarity and precluded the possibility of internal dissension and abrupt social change. See Konrad Lorenz, <u>On Aggression.</u>

The Haidas, who were neighbors of the Nootka, were not as solipsistic as their head hunting cousins. The purpose of war for the Haida was to acquire wealth. Murdock called them the Vikings of the Northwest coast. Like the Vikings, they would rather have taken enemies as slaves than as trophies. These slaves added to the wealth of the tribe and were used as trading tokens with other Indian groups. However, the enemies who were killed in raids were beheaded. The heads were stuck on poles, returned to the home camp and used in a victory dance.

The practical economics of the Haida precluded a holocaust approach to their enemies. Aspirations to wealth and power required certain reliance upon acceptable tokens of trade. The Vikings recognized this factor and often limited their head hunting to the most valiant or noble of the enemy. Constantine Poryphyrogentius reported an incident in 972 AD, which reflects this attitude. The Petchenegs, who were enemies of the Rus Vikings, defeated the Rus in battle. As a symbol of their power they killed the Viking Prince Svyatoslav and made a drinking vessel of his skull. They were, however, too practical a people to have done this with the skull of every Viking prisoner. Prisoners were tokens of wealth and trade. The Scythians took the same approach. Although they were known to use heads in victory celebrations and to make drinking cups from skulls, the bulk of their prisoners they used as slaves. Slaves were used throughout their domains as legal tender.

The natural euphoric feeling caused by head hunting sometimes engendered a sense of guilt and uneasiness. The hunter often experienced a feeling of being unclean after he had killed and decapitated an enemy. Among his own people, killing a fellow tribesman would have been considered taboo. The killing of an enemy was not taboo but still left him with the same sense of shame. The adulation of victory could rapidly give way to a sense of anxiety and despair.

It is the very nature of taboo that generates this feeling. Freud suggested that taboo represented a conflict between the individual and authority. In adhering to the taboo the individual was required to renounce his inclination to do something that he really wanted to do. The primary taboo, such as the one against murder, established the relationship between members. A rebellion against its law would create social disharmony and possibly social disintegration. The same feeling was aroused by the deliberate death of a foe. A sense of despair, born of a certain loss of social consciousness, caused this phenomenon. See Sigmund Freud, Totem and Taboo.

To rid themselves of this uneasy sensation the hunters subjected themselves to various purification rituals. Typically, these rites demanded isolation of the warrior from the group, abstinence from intercourse with women, social as well as sexual, and the severe restriction of diet. Some of these observed practices required the devotee to spend extended periods of time engaged in purification. The Natchez Indians of North America purified themselves for as long as six months. Freud suggested that the victim was taboo from the moment of his death and that the taboo was extended to every item the victim had touched and every action he had committed. The extension of taboo was combined with a fear of the victim's ghost. The enemy might have been dead but his mana was still strong enough to bring harm to the victor or the victor's family. The lustrations performed were necessary to destroy the power of the dead man's mana.

Often the hunter expressed a feeling of anxiety over the fate of the heads taken in battle. The inhabitants of the Island of Timor experienced such concern. These people made elaborate efforts to "appease" the head. Delicacies from the tribal food supply were proffered to the skull. The hunters implored forgiveness for the enemy's death. Some attempts were made to convert the spirit of the victim that he might accept his new "home." The supplicants asked the spirit to forsake his former tribe and friends and to join the new tribe. Sir James George Frazer believed that this was simply representative of the fear of the dead man's ghost. Freud, however, suggested that the reason was more complex. The hunters had more than a simple hatred and fear of the hunted. They also had admiration and respect for the warrior. The invitation to join the new community, in spirit, may well have been made out of a sense of warrior community, one that transcended tribal or group loyalties.

This practice reaffirms the suggestion by Levi-Strauss that ethnocentrically isolated peoples had a speculative attitude toward death. They believed that they could make a deal with the spirits of the departed on a "quid pro quo" basis. This is why the Celts put the heads of their enemies on poles above their chimneys. The skull would protect the household in exchange for its own preservation. It would not be destroyed and lost to memory. The ritual was common among the Hopi Indians whose fighters only took the scalp from the head. The Hopi clansman was confined to the Kiva, a sacred meeting place, for twenty days following a raiding party. At the end of this Vegismal period a dance was held around the pole on which his scalps were hung. The scalps were thrown into a rock fissure at the conclusion of the dance. Every evening corn meal was thrown into the fissure to "propitiate" the scalps. The spirits of the dead must be appeased. This ritual was continued as long as one of the warriors from the raiding party was still alive, even after long years.

For the warrior the integrative value of head hunting was a two edged sword. The taking of heads in battle was a mechanism whereby the warrior society was drawn together and given a sense of accomplishment. This was particularly the case when the head of an important and powerful enemy was displayed. On the other side of the scale was the effect upon the cult when one of its own important members lost his head to an enemy. What happens when the enemy forces display such trophies to our group? Undoubtedly the effect was a disaster of unsettling proportions. The Moslem invasion of Hindu India in 1565 AD provides an illuminating example. The last Hindu stronghold of Vijayanagar was besieged by Moslem artillery. During a Hindu attack, the Moslems captured the Raja whose head they removed and displayed to the Hindus. The result was total panic on the part of the Hindu cavalry. A complete rout ensued. See Campbell, The Masks of God.

As a cultural option the headhunting raid was, if not universal, very widespread. The attention paid to skulls in prehistoric settings, to the exclusion of the skeleton, suggests that the practice was an integral part of human cultural development. Did most societies pass through a head hunting "phase"? Was that developmental phase a result of cultural diffusion or independent invention? There are no particular ecological elements that would help in answering these questions. Backtracking from more current primitive cultures seems the only valid approach. There is the Freudian analysis that head hunting was an infantile fixation of some kind. Money-Kyrle postulated this approach in the 1930s when discussing human sacrifice. The arguments are unconvincing.

Analysis of the cultural selection factor points to the transitional phases between the use of head hunting as a ritual and the use of decapitation as a punishment. By the time of the Persian Empire beheading was no longer a strictly ritual function among civilized peoples. If head hunting were a universal practice it follows that the breakup of holistic communal enterprises, a dissolution resulting from social stratification, might have channeled the practice into more specific uses such as criminal justice. The practice was not necessarily limited to punishment in these stratified cultures. With the development of economic systems in which one could aspire to considerable wealth, the head, as a symbol of warrior status, would have become functionally meaningless. War in this case would be a very specialized endeavor not always involving the entire community or necessarily threatening its existence.

Head hunting played a role in the Warrior's confrontation with the problem of impermanence. Attempts to appease the skull and cajole its spirit into joining the tribe reflect the concern of the victor over his own fate should he fall prey to conquest. His enemies might reciprocate the strict observance on his part of rituals regarding the heads that he had taken in battle. A kind of "Geneva Convention" of headhunters might agree to observe the "rules." Professional courtesy, even among the most isolated and primitive people, is to be expected.

For the Celts, the opposite was true. Their head hunting reflected a simple desire to upstage their foes. The practice was also exercised to prevent the enemy from being a further problem. The Celt believed in reincarnation. Warriors died and were reborn into the same tribe to fight again. The only stipulation regarding rebirth was that the warrior be intact. If the Celts took and kept the heads of their enemies, the enemies would not be reborn. They had taken that part of the foe that held his spirit captive. An enemy so captured and contained was one less with which to contend in the next generation of fighters.

The relationship between self-esteem and head hunting should be obvious. The captured skull, whether drinking cup or talisman, was the appropriate mark of honor. The intense feeling of power, which accompanied the successful raider, spilled over into all other aspects of his life. It made him a person to be reckoned with. The man whose skill in war won him an appropriate place in the cultural hierarchy was one who had garnered the fullest measure of self-esteem.

The Demonstration of Power

In Lewis Carol's story about <u>Alice in Wonderland</u> he wrote about a spiteful queen called the Queen of Hearts. Her reaction to almost everyone was disagreeable. Her favorite expression was "off with their heads." His story may have been a fantasy but the characterization of monarchs with similar personalities was quite accurate. The phrase "off with their heads" has been more than a casual response of many monarchs.

In his wanderings through the literature of Brazil Claude Levi-Strauss found evidence of such a playing card aristocracy. This culture flourished at the time of the Portuguese explorations. The tribe in question was called the Mbaya-guacura. They were a "master race" that had imposed a military hegemony on central Brazil. Their subject peoples were used for the service and sport of the aristocracy. The warriors brought home the heads of enemies. Levi-Strauss said that the queen of these people, like the Queen of Hearts, was fond of playing with these heads as though they were toys. In their feasts they used the heads as drinking vessels. If there were a shortage of "cups" for the guests the queen might say, simply, of the nearest servants, "off with their heads."

The point of all this discussion about Alice and her friends is quite simple. Head hunting was often used as a demonstration of power. This was not the kind of power that a warrior demonstrated over his opponent by defeating him in battle. This was the kind of power that the representative of constituted authority demonstrated over his people. To be able to demand, at will, the head of anyone of her subjects, was to have a license for the queen to kill. We would think of the Queen of Hearts and her colleagues as despots who simply abused authority for their own pleasure. However, the incidence of this practice was carried from one generation to the next and beheading in this manner and for this reason became a customary practice. The assessment of despotism must be tempered by tradition.

These beheadings took place most frequently among those peoples whose cultural aim was to please the monarch. The practice was quite frequent in the Eastern World. Among the Persians it was customary to offer the king a present from time to time. The most appropriate gift was always the head of one of the king's enemies. In an area where the political fortunes of a soldier were determined by the whimsy of despotism and where enemies were made and unmade with a thought the custom obviously grew to magnanimous proportions.

There is no more poignant an example of this sycophancy than that of Nero Caesar who, in addition to being paranoid, was an avid fan of cloak and dagger. In 62 AD, according to Tacitus, two Roman nobles, Plautus and Sulla, were murdered on the order of the emperor. This was done because Nero believed that the two were plotting against him. The heads of both men were severed and brought to the emperor for inspection. Nero made jeering remarks about the heads while expressing wonder that he, Nero, could ever have been afraid of such fellows. Naturally the agents of this dark deed were standing by awaiting their reward.

Nero extended this paranoia into his own family. In order to marry his mistress, Poppea, he had to get rid of his wife, Octavia. He believed that Octavia was plotting against him. Nero ordered her execution. When Octavia had been dispatched her head was removed and returned to her rival, Poppea. Tacitus called this act a "refinement of cruelty." Nero played this little game countless times. His executions are an example of a practice that is characteristic of many autocracies. An imagined fear creates a need for the death of an innocent party and the subsequent abuse of the lifeless corpse for the amusement of the crowd.

Sometimes the fears were not imagined and the enemies were real. After the death of Cyrus of Persia the Persian priests took over the government. These Magi, as they were called, instituted a new religious order that the old nobility saw as a threat to their position. The nobles fostered a revolution in which a young man named Darius figured prominently. The Magi were easily overthrown and the confederates of Darius, who was soon to be emperor, ran through the streets waving the heads of the Magi. This head waving ritual was meant as a sign of the new king's power.

The Massagetae, a tribe related to the Scythians, had killed this same Cyrus in Egypt. It seems that the leader of this tribe had several children. Cyrus had wantonly killed them before a battle. In retaliation the chief of the Massagetae found the body of Cyrus, cut off the head and kept the head in a wineskin filed with human blood. The head of the Persian "King of kings" in a blood filled wineskin was testimony to the power of this nomadic tribe of warriors. See Herodotus, The Histories.

Perhaps the best demonstration of power is that of the victor who can display the heads of his enemies when those enemies are known for their ferocity and martial zeal. The Vikings were such a fierce and zealous band of warriors. As they were known for the "Berserk" and an almost invincible strength and courage, they were the object of much curiosity in captivity. The general who could produce a number of Viking heads on his belt was an accomplished warrior, worthy of every epithet. In 844 AD such a general made his debut. Abd Al Rahman, the Emir of Seville, defeated the Viking raiders at Talayata. In addition to sinking thirty of the famous Viking warships, he captured many prisoners. Most of these were hanged. He reserved two hundred to be decapitated. The heads were sent to Tangiers where they were displayed as a symbol of the Emir's power over his enemies. The Emir understood the value of such demonstrations. Such examples kept his vassals in line with policy. What he could do to an enemy such as the Vikings he could also do to one of his own subjects.

There are many examples of the autocratic uses of head hunting. There are far too many to render even a representative sample. In the evolutionary development of ritual into ideology, which challenges the holistic view of life, this style of head hunting represents a transitional phase. Where the simple society seeks integration the more complex one seeks control. Where the simple society seeks a cultural option the complex insists upon a behavioral necessity. In this instance death had become a regulatory agent of behavior rather than a part of culture. Esteem had become personally exclusive.

Religion and Death

We have discussed at length the Andaman Islanders who exhumed the bones of their dead after the flesh had decayed. The skull and lower jaw were preserved and were both dyed red and white. The appropriate relatives wore these skulls. A woman wore the skull of her husband, a mother that of her child. The Andamaners placed much importance upon the preservation of these skulls. The effect was communal rather than individual. In fact, they traded these skulls with one another. The skull which one displayed as a pendant or charm might not be that of his ancestor. One might say that the ancestor worship of an Andamaner was communal.

The case of the Andaman Islanders exemplifies the use of the head in religious and magical practices. Much of this was centered on the worship of ancestors. Ancestor worship accomplished three things. First it made a connection between the living and the dead. Second it provided a continuity of tradition from one generation to the next by giving each new group a heritage to revere. Third, ancestor worship provided a focal point for the cohesion of the social structure. All of these factors were important in maintaining a healthy and vibrant social life within the communities that practiced them. So important were these rituals to some communities that the absence or diminution of these rites caused the very communities to die out. Many of the primitive tribes, once affected by Christianity, lost all of their old beliefs and practices, almost overnight. In the analysis of the skull as a part of magic, religion and death, this section will consider ancestor worship as an integral part of social well being.

Ancestor worship was sometimes restricted to cult worship. In the Solomon Islands a great chief, upon his demise, often became the object of cult worship. His mourners placed his head and bones in a specially constructed house. In that place they venerated his remains. The veneration was thought to affect the fortunes of the tribe. The skull of the chief was given credit for good fortune and blame for bad fortune. Interest in his shrine waxed and waned with the coming and passing of good fortune. During times of great prosperity the memory of the chief and strict attention to the adoration of his skull was passed on to succeeding generations as long as his family continued to produce descendants. The importance of the skull was sufficient to make its shrine the center of village life and activity over multiple generations of time and people.

Other groups practiced this skull cult in a very similar manner. We have discussed, in chapter one, the Manus of Melanesia, who preserved the skull of the male head of household until the death of the son.

Herodotus mentioned a people called the Issodones who preserved the skull of their fathers. They offered sacrifice to these skulls as a commemoration of their owners' lives and also to request favors of the ancestral spirits. As these people offered human sacrifices to their gods it may be assumed that they sacrificed humans to their ancestors as well. Herodotus also reported that the Scythians used the skulls of their departed brothers in a commemorative manner. This included the decoration of the skull with leather or gold and its use as a drinking cup. The skull was brought out on special occasions and put to these uses. The Scythians boasted of the merits of their dead kinsmen in the same manner that they boasted of the defeat over their enemies. They brought out the heads of those subjects and used the skulls as conversational gambits.

Among the people who paid special attention to the skull of their king or chief was the Cocam of Maya Pan. These tribesmen removed the flesh of their dead kings by boiling. The skull was saved and turned into a mask. This mask represented the departed monarch. It was also used on ceremonial occasions and was venerated as one of the family gods of the Cocam. Curiously, no other people in Meso-America used the skull as an object of ancestor worship. It was unique to the Cocam.

This preservation of the skull was a religious and magical practice that emphasized the recognition of death and the possibility of preserving life after death. Many of these practices reflected a religious dualism in which nature went beyond the grave and involved both good and evil. The good and evil could be confronted by the living, especially by a communal action. In Polynesia, the head of a chief was sometimes preserved because of the mana it was thought to possess. In this instance mana was a kind of currency with which good fortune might be purchased. Sacrificial victims were thought to give up their mana when they died. The sacrifice officials used the mana to purchase good luck for a major societal undertaking. The interesting part of this use of mana was the association of evil manna with flesh and good mana with bone. Perhaps good mana was thought to reside in bone because bone lasts longer than flesh.

These practices, in which attention is paid to the skull of ancestors, involve a major consideration of this essay. Man has a confrontation with the problem of impermanence and needs control over his environment and his destiny. The practice of ancestor worship and head hunting is in support of that confrontation with death. The magical and religious aspects of the practice reinforce the sense of control. The Jivaro of Ecuador, for example, believed that the shrunken heads that they processed had a magical power that could affect increase in the fields. The successful headhunter took his trophies to the fields where he performed ceremonies for the success of cultivated crops and pigs and other domestic animals. This may seem to have little to do with the problem of death. One must recognize how precarious a balance exists in a primitive community. When one sees that these people believed in the currency of the shrunken heads' mana it is easy to understand the connection between the practice and the view of life and death.

The religious aspects of head hunting also extended to the warrior. The warrior societies, whose preoccupation with life were always to include recognition of the immanence of death, used heads in their religious aspirations. The Aztecs, who made war to gain captives for sacrifice, kept head racks for the display of slain captives. Hays suggested that his practice was a malevolent distortion of the sexuality associated with head hunting. Whatever the Freudian analysis the religious intent was obvious, if only that the heads were intended to serve as a tangible display of worship. The Thracians were less subtle in their ceremonies. Livy says that the Thracian warriors raised the heads of their slain opponents on spear points as an offering to the god of war.

In her marvelous book, Patterns of Culture, Ruth Benedict has suggested that head hunting was a challenge to the affront of death. She described the reaction of a Kwakiutl Indian chief to the death of his son. Rather than shed tears of lamentation, the chief went to a neighboring village, accosted its chief, killed him and took his head. This head taking was a way of getting back at death for taking his own son. Among these tribes this sort of ritual was obligatory.

The integrative function of head hunting served to solidify community endeavors, where those endeavors sought to contend with the problems of religion and death. Cultural selection established procedures whereby those endeavors might make sense to the practitioners. The trend seems to have favored the veneration of the father as the head of the household. As patriarch he was rightfully entitled to the respect due his position. The problem of impermanence was met by simply according to the head or skull those qualities that needed to be preserved. This preservation justified the existence and function of the community.

As a religious object the head was most certainly a token or esteem. Perhaps the most revered of the body parts, its use served to recognize the value of sense perception in man, senses that are generated and controlled by the head. It may have been primitive and grotesque, but it was, in a sense, a kind of social progress. "Alas, poor Yorick, I knew him well."

Cannibals

Like head hunting, cannibalism was an attempt to preserve the mana and, generally, the desirable qualities of the deceased. Cannibalism was a demonstration of power over an enemy. In fact, when one practice was indulged the other was usually present in some form. This is particularly true of the relationship between headhunting and brain cannibalism. One was practiced to support the other. Among some peoples cannibalism was also a source of dietary supplement. Although hunting of humans for food was very limited we shall deal with its occurrence briefly to demonstrate its occurrence and the lack of ritual which accompanied the practice.

Most of the examples of cannibalism as a dietary supplement come from Africa and Polynesia where the availability of other forms of animal flesh are severely restricted by ecological factors. Some examples, however, are different in that they illustrate man and his attitudes at the beginning of his cultural development. For purposes of illustration the habits of Sinanthropus, or Peking Man, and some of the Neolithic peoples of the upper Danube area shall be used to demonstrate this level of cultural development. These instances are not inclusive. Rather they are representative of the food gathering aspects of the cannibal art.

Peking Man was discovered in a cave in Northern China. Along with this Sinanthropus were the bones of forty other hominids that had apparently been killed by Peking Man. Howell suggested that many of the hominid bones exhibited evidence of cannibalism. Human teeth made the teeth marks on the human bones. As Sinanthropus was at least five hundred thousand years old the evidence suggests that the practice of cannibalism among hominids is very ancient.

Was the practice ritual? The cultural development of man in China over half a million years ago was probably not sufficient to provide any meaningful ritual activity. Culture of any merit did not come to the area until about 1200 BC. There is another, archeological factor, which suggests the absence of ritual. Sinanthropus left behind in his caves the bones of numerous animals scattered among the human bones. It may be that he did not discriminate between man and animal at his level of culture. It may also be that game was seasonal and that human food was necessary to provide him with flesh during the hard times. The evidence, although not conclusive, suggests this probability.

The second example of anthropophagous activity as a dietary supplement is one that occurred among the farming peoples of the upper Danube in the Neolithic period. These people were obviously much more cultured than was Sinanthropus. In Rumania, excavators found a child's bones and another skull, not that of the child, in the midst of a hearth which was littered with numerous animal bones. The disregard for the child in relation to the animal bones suggested to Johannes Maringer that the child had been eaten along with the animals. Apparently it was the evidence of the child having been eaten (teeth marks) that kept Maringer from supposing that the child had been buried in the hearth with the animals. Many peoples have been buried with animals of one kind or another. The Scythians were buried with horses. The Iranians were buried in the floor of the house, underneath the hearth. But this child was decidedly a victim of cannibalism.

The most common kind of cannibalism was that which was truly a ritual. Only a portion of the deceased was eaten. The exception to this was endocannibalistic burial. In endocannibalism the intent was to preserve the qualities of the deceased by ingesting his body. One very peculiar form of this practice was observed by the so-called slash and burn societies of South East Asia. These people cremated their dead, mixed the ashes with a fermented drink and drank the mixture. As the ashes of the cut down trees were necessary to the growth of new plants it followed logically that they had some vital force which could make the earth spring to life again. This was the same vital force that the living plant possessed. From this they deduced that the same was true of people. If the ashes of the deceased were consumed then the consumer would imbibe the vitality of the dead person.

Herodotus told a story about the same kind of practice among the Issodones. When a man's father died, his kinsmen came to his house with a sheep. This animal was slaughtered and offered to the gods. The sheep was then cut into small portions. The body of the deceased was treated in a similar fashion. Then the two were mixed together and the relatives of the dead man ate the flesh. The Issodones were apparently concerned with the preservation of their ancestral lines. Thus they ingested their forbears.

One has to be wary of these accounts by Herodotus. The historian was widely traveled and had a keen eye but he was also given to exaggeration and to ascribing to many different peoples the same attributes. He told a similar tale of the Massagetae. They included all of their old people in a sacrifice of cattle. Humans were cut up in small parts and eaten along with the beef. Apparently the old people knew when it was their time to be sacrificed. A man was considered disgraced if he were killed or died of disease and did not live long enough to be sacrificed. This story sounds almost unreal. Herodotus does say that the Massagetae did not eat the bodies of those who had died of disease. He mentioned also the Callatiae, neighbors of the Greeks, who ate the bodies of their dead parents.

It is quite possible that many of these stories have a grain of truth. Perhaps they ate only a portion of the body in a symbolic gesture toward the ancestors. The practice of serving dead bodies to those who had displeased a monarch was known among the Persians. The practice among the peoples described by Herodotus was, perhaps, partly real and partly a good story for the chronicler and his readers. But the practice of partial cannibalistic consumption was real enough.

The Arunta of Australia indulged themselves in endocannibalism in a ceremonial way during initiation rites and as a cure for physical weakness among older children. During these rites, in which a young Arunta boy was circumcised, his younger brother was made to eat the prepuce, or foreskin, of the initiate. This prepuce was supposed to have made the young boy grow faster so that he could take his place in the adult, male world. In the same vein a younger child was occasionally killed and fed to an older, weaker child. This was not done just to feed the older child but to give him the qualities of the stronger, younger child.

Another form of this practice included drinking the blood of a kinsman in the swearing of oaths. The Greeks, Celts and Scythians practiced this kind of oath swearing. The Greeks even licked the cuts they made in one another's arms to seal the bond. These and other rituals indicate that the main motivation behind endocannibalism was to establish a connection with one's own group and the solidarity of its purpose. In these practices there exists, on the part of practitioners, an awareness of tradition and history in which the continuity of generations was established. Rather than allow the virtues of an individual to be dissipated into the earth and thus diminish the overall spiritual strength of the community, the virtues were ingested. The idea of the resurrection of the body was not considered because these peoples were too closely attached to the mother earth and the cycles of nature.

In exocannibalism the intent was the same except that the virtues of someone outside the tribe were sought for preservation. In the logic of the ethnocentric this was a better kind of preservation because it was possible to add to the virtue of the community. Endocannibalism could, at best, only establish a balance between the living and the dead. The spiritual substance of the community could not be increased from within. It may be argued that a community could increase its spiritual substance by increasing its population through live birth. Most of these peoples, however, believed that the newborn child was a reincarnation of a distant ancestor. The next best way to increase the spiritual substance was by adoption. Cannibalism was such a method.

In Polynesia, where human sacrifice was used to release mana from the body, brain cannibalism and the eating of the heart were practiced as a way of ingesting mana. The Aztecs often ate the bodies of victims who had been sacrificed to the gods. The bodies of outstanding warriors were considered to be the best. The Witoto of the Amazon practiced a similar ritual in which internal organs, such as the heart and liver, were mixed with tobacco juice and eaten raw. These practices were justified by the worshipers as being the best way to increase their own prowess and strength.

The loss of a relative or friend within some groups caused a military action to get underway, this to restore the mana that had been lost. The Tupi-Guarani of South America had elaborate rituals in which a war captive was executed in revenge of the death of a tribal relative. This was done with great ceremony, including play and dance on the part of the condemned. The victim was killed with a club. His flesh was cooked and eaten. Sometimes, before the captive was killed, he was offered the flesh of another victim. The most demonstrative part of the ceremony, with respect to the replacement of spiritual substance (other than the cannibal act itself), was the dressing of the condemned in the attire of the dead relative for whom he was being killed. The captive, before his death, was made a surrogate relative, a member of the tribe. This same tendency existed in head hunting where the enemy head was invited to join the new tribe. The Hopi and the Celts, two disparate peoples, practiced this kind of entreaty before the heads of those they killed in battle

Cannibalism was also considered a source of magic. Among the Pijan of the Andes the bodies of enemies were the principal source of magical power. When an enemy was not available a noteworthy member of the Pijan warriors volunteered himself. He willingly allowed himself to be killed and eaten so that others of the tribe could benefit from the magic and power of his body. Some of the modern day Voodoo practices evolved from the cannibalistic ways of the Pijan.

The Kwakiutl Indians practiced a ritual form of cannibalism in one of their secret societies. This society was called the Cannibals. They worshipped a god known as Cannibal who lived at the North End of the World. All candidates for membership were required to chew upon human flesh during their initiation. They were often required to bite chunks of flesh from the arms of onlookers. What marked the successful candidate was his supposed passion for human flesh. This passionate hunger was acquired from his devotion to the Cannibal at the North End of the World. Even so, the Kwakiutl had a loathing for cannibalism. They therefore restricted the activities of the Cannibal Society to specific public ceremonies that were spaced more than four years apart. The new Cannibals were required to undergo strict purification rituals that could go on for years. The Cannibal was never allowed to actually swallow the flesh that he chewed upon. Still he was allowed to chew upon the flesh of a suitable corpse. This was meant to connect the living and dead elements of the society. The practice was meant to create a balance between the active cultural life of the community and its inherent spirituality.

There is no doubt that cannibalism and head hunting had an integrative function among Ethnocentrics. There is little question that cultural selection was instrumental in regulating the life of individuals within the community. The relation to the problem of impermanence, especially among very undeveloped tribes should be obvious. In spite of all of this and in spite of the attachment to the cycles of nature that these peoples shared there remains a question. How could one man kill and eat another except under the direst circumstances? This is more than a question of difference between Western culture and any other culture. It is a fundamental problem to all human societies. There were, after all, many such societies that never practiced cannibalism.

Konrad Lorenz made one suggestion in his book <u>On Aggression</u>. His argument is that the peoples who engaged in cannibalism were controlled by what he called Psuedo-speciation. That is to say that they did not consider other peoples to be humans but rather considered them to be animals. It is easy to kill and eat someone who is only considered another source of game or at least subhuman. It must be noted that many of the peoples who did not practice cannibalism believed that their neighbors were inferior to themselves.

Another argument is that life, to the ethnocentric, belonged to culture rather than to nature. What a man did and how he lived were functions of the group in which he dwelled. When a person died his death was considered an affront to culture because the substance of the community was altered and diminished. Cannibalism was a way of preserving culture through the recognition that life and the qualities of life. Cannibalism, in that it sought to preserve the good qualities of people, was an effort to increase and develop culture.

A third factor is the practice of cannibalism as a demonstration of power over an enemy. The partaken flesh was a token of esteem for the individual to show that he had killed his enemy. The cannibal act was his way of showing to the rest of his tribe the position that he had attained by his valor. The fact that it was mostly men and mostly warriors who were the cannibals attests to this warrior cult aspect of cannibalism. Power meant that there was spiritual substance and social recognition achieved through the act.

There are many instances of this warrior pride among the so-called primitive peoples. However, one of the more bizarre twists to this demonstration of power was that practiced by peoples who had abhorrence for human flesh. In this case esteem was gained by forcing someone else, not always with an immediate knowledge, to consume human flesh. In this case the enforcer of the feast had a great loathing for the intended consumer. For purposes of illustration we shall use several examples from Herodotus who, apparently, loved to ascribe these bizarre practices to anyone who had the misfortune of not having been born a Greek.

Astyages was a Persian ruler. He had a chief servant named Harpagus to whom he entrusted a very delicate mission. It seems that the king was afraid of his, that is the king's, newborn son. He thought that someday the boy would overthrow him. So he ordered Harpagus to kill the boy and make the murder seem like an accident. Harpagus, who was not an evil sort of person, could not carry out the order. Instead he deceived the king. He did this by substituting the body of a stillborn infant. Then he gave the king's son to a shepherd. This story is probably not exactly true since the theme occurs so often in the mythology of the East. Some years later Cyrus, the king's son, and later, emperor, came to the attention of Astyges and the king realized that he had been deceived. Harpagus must be punished.

Harpagus also had a son, born about the same time as Cyrus. The king had this son killed and butchered. He ordered the parts to be cooked and served to Harpagus at a great feast. This dinner was ostensibly given in the honor of Harpagus. After the king's minister had eaten as much as he could, the king asked if Harpagus were satisfied with the meal. Harpagus responded that indeed he was. The king next ordered that the head of Harpagus' son be served. When the head was shown to Harpagus, Astyages asked him if he were still satisfied with the dinner. Harpagus, who knew that a negative reply would result in his own death, replied affirmatively. This practice of punishment, according to Herodotus, was common among the Persian rulers. It was a demonstration of their absolute power over their subjects. That a monarch could command another person to consume his own flesh and blood and then to say that he had enjoyed doing so is a considerable measure of power.

The Greek historian accuses the Scythians of a similar practice. Some of these Scythians were appointed to guard and train some Persian youths. Cyaxares, the king of the Medes, had great confidence in the hunting prowess of the Scythians. One day they returned from the field without any game and the king was filled with anger. He fell to ridiculing the Scythians in front of the young Persian boys. In retaliation the warriors killed one of their pupils, cooked the body and had it served to the king. Then they fled before the atrocity could be discovered. This deed was their way of showing contempt and revenge toward a monarch who had made jest of their skills as hunters and warriors.

These rituals, however gruesome, were limited to specific instances in which the barbaric pride of individuals got in the way of ordinary social custom. In a sense they represent a transitional phase from true ritual and may more properly reflect an ideological inhumanity. Yet they were frequent enough to be considered customary among certain peoples and among certain cultural subgroups.

Cannibalism, in whatever form, was a measure of esteem for the individual and his group. The willingness of the cannibal to treat the body of another as a source of spiritual substance reflects his desire to increase his own measure of worth. Yet the act was a temperate one because its purpose was symbolic rather than dietary. The goal was the sustenance of esteem.

# 6

## *That Old Time Religion*

No one can be certain at what point the first hominid became the first thinking individual or if that propitious moment occurred more than once. Perhaps it is a moot point to ponder stages in the evolution of the intellect. The important fact is that such a moment did take place and marked the beginning of cultural development. Man became aware of himself as a person, of having surroundings separate from his own personality. He discovered his ability to relate to others of his kind. His interactions reached beyond the immediate demands of nature. That is not to say that language, or any other form of communication, was spontaneous with the development and use of intellect. The seed was planted. Man had begun to develop cultural awareness that was to lead him into the use of ritual in his dealings with the world. Teilhard de Chardin would say that man, after having imitated the development of nature, proceeded to develop his own separate and psychosocial convolution through a process of "Complexification" that became a synergistic expression of his very development. See Teilhard de Chardin, The Phenomenon of Man.

The above paragraph may seem very pedestrian, very obvious and without any literary or historical merit. The fact is that thirty thousand years ago man possessed the same intelligence and abilities as our own. His genius would have been able to accommodate the subtleties of nuclear fission or architectural engineering as readily as any modern day intellect might understand them. What he lacked was the intellectual toolbox, not the intellectual talent, to do the job. With the historical and cultural awareness of modern man he would have performed as well, or as poorly, as modern man. One need only look at the mathematics developed by the ancient Greeks to recognize that intellectual capacity and its expression are not dependent upon sophisticated technology.

The substance of this intellectual capacity and its various applications became sufficiently obvious to early man that he could develop very simple ritual in his everyday life. These rituals, which initially paid attention to nature, gave him a sense of his cultural circumstances. Through this ritual he could pass on his own cultural sense to his descendants. The ritual became significant because the world of culture was preserved through its reenactment. The reenactment of the ritual, always an imperfect duplication, supported change and the consequent acceleration of cultural evolution. Awareness precipitated cultural evolution that caused a greater awareness that precipitated a kind of snowball effect that continues to our own day. The reader is cautioned that the process is more exponential, or of a quantum nature, than linear and that there have been many instances of cultural regression and annihilation. The net balance, however, has sustained a synergistic and an anabolic process.

The development and refinement of ritual relied upon the order and harmony that man found about him. Most behaviorists would agree that the cognitive domain of the human organism relies upon a system of categorization, one that needs a label for practically everything. The most startling discovery that a young child makes is that everything has a name. This cognitive domain in early man was able to recognize that the order and harmony in nature might be duplicated by ritual. Many rituals attempted to imitate nature or some vital part of man's role in nature.

In his attempt to reproduce the natural order which he had perceived he developed the use of sympathetic magic. Religion was a logical next step. There has been considerable argument about the provenance of magic and religion. Which one arrived first? Is one simply a distortion of the other? For our purposes we shall restrict the problem to the uses of these practices in establishing a sense of order. Many rituals were intended to recognize and to insure the continence of the order and harmony in the universe. The Aztecs spent thousands of lives every year that they might "feed" the sun and thus keep it from falling out of the sky. The Hindus made their sacrifices to Kali, the Earth Mother, so that she could continue to insure the cycles of nature and the regular order and harmony of the seasons.

The cycles of nature were detected because of their regularity. Where that regularity was observed ritual sprang up as a complement to man's reliance upon the perennial nature of nature. The Egyptians, and all river peoples, developed innumerable rituals regarding the gods and the forces of the river. In chapter three we discussed some of the ways in which humans were sacrificed to mollify water gods of one kind or another. Water, which is a universal necessity to life on earth and usually a threat to that life as flooding, was one of the main objects and sources of ritual development. No doubt many an unfortunate victim was offered to the river or water god to insure a bountiful supply but not a torrential destruction. Order and harmony reinforced the practice and significance of ritual long after its origins had vanished.

As man developed his sense of cultural awareness his intellectual tools were honed. Language and other communication were made more precise and definitive. The use of language allowed the oral transmission of history and tradition. Language was, in fact, the only means by which this history could be passed down. Ethnocentrics had a keen sense of tradition and knew the value of recording and passing that lore to new generations accurately. Many tribes had sages whose sole function was to learn by heart the history of the clan so that the knowledge would not be lost. Such historians relied upon songs, chants, stories and the ritual reenactment of historical events to insure the continuity of the tradition.

Ritual was most important in this reenactment of history. The Polynesian chief whose bones were venerated belonged to this ritual reenactment. His family preserved the exploits of the chief; those achieved in war or peace. The stories were told and retold to his descendants for as long as his genetic line survived. The same was true of the Muisca king whose bones were preserved in a special shrine and whose entire mummified body was carried into battle. The Siberian Shaman was an object of veneration. The children of the deceased and distant ancestor found a sense of tradition and history in stories about their antecedent. Without ritual these people would have lost most of their folklore. Their cultural progress would have been diminished.

The sense of having a history and following tradition in accord with rigid guidelines gave the tribe a sense of being special. The rites set them apart from other tribes whose members had no such history. This probably contributed to the development of racial prejudices and what Konrad Lorenz called pseudo-speciation. That is sometimes a negative factor in the establishment of intense community loyalties. This sense of community, however, allowed individuals to work together to fulfill what they considered to be their goals, those defined by their history, culture and tradition. The main significance of ritual in this instance was that it helped to preserve both the history and the tradition of the community.

Ritual was also important because it had a regulatory function. The social obligations of the individual were defined by the role he played in those rituals that were performed by the group. There are many examples in the texts that reinforce this fact. A Scythian, in order to become a full-fledged member of the tribe, must take a head in battle. The Arunta boy, to prove his manhood, was required to subincise his genital organs. The Aztec worshiper was expected to mortify his flesh by letting blood from his own veins and by running a string of thorns through a hole in his tongue. All of these examples point to the significance of ritual as an agent of social control. The ordinary individual was compelled by ritual to abide by the "rules of the game."

Ritual was not only designed to create a set of obligations for the individual but was also designed to regulate the manner and time in which these obligations should be met. The intricate systems of taboo, which existed among many primitives, suggest that ritual observance be designed to effect complete control over any individual life. After killing an enemy in war, the Hopi Indian was confined to his Kiva for a period of twenty days. Among many warrior cults there were certain prayers that were said, certain foods that were not eaten and certain people with whom verbal and physical communication was not allowed. A man could not have access to his wife in many instances during these periods.

Among civilized societies ritual was an even more important factor in the regulation of social life. Those civilizations that had the ability to write were able to more precisely define the manner in which ceremony could be performed and by whom. The rise of a priestly class supported this regulation. In Rome, Egypt and China the priests and scribes were the recorders and interpreters of ritual. Often the only people who could read and write were the scribes and priests. Their special position allowed them to "create" religion and ritual. Simply "editing" the sacred writings could effect change. This precise definition, however determined, was to affect the course of culture because it was as good as law. In many cases it was the only law.

The goal of ritual was to develop a sense of cultural awareness, incorporating the order and harmony of the universe. Tradition and history both reinforced this written and oral awareness. The end result was to establish regulatory mechanisms with which to manage society. These factors were supported by a continuous flow of instructions from one generation to the next and by the consistent reenactment of the very history represented by ritual. The practices of suttee and human sacrifice were largely state controlled enterprises which most often reinforced the position of people in their own society. The social order determined the respective roles of the participants. The use of ornaments and the practices of head hunting and cannibalism were much more holistic and integrative arts. They reflect the attributes of simpler societies in which the state functions were really in the hands of the majority. The important point is that ritual and its development were imperative to the growth of culture.

The objection will be raised that many of the rituals discussed in this book were extremely barbaric and, from the Western viewpoint, entirely unnecessary. The source of the objection is obviously modern and Western. The fact is that ethnocentric peoples have always recognized existence as a very immediate, a very imperative and a very vibrant fact. The rituals concerning life and its sustenance must be equal to the task of survival. No half measures were allowed. If a fault existed then the fault was a lack of understanding, not a dearth of human feelings or good intentions. These ethnocentric peoples indulged in savage practices without having to consider themselves as savages. They were close to nature and saw in nature a violent but vigorous force. The description of the goddess Kali in chapter five is typical of this early view of nature. Those who indulged the barbaric were not barbarians. They were everyday folks looking for meaning, substance and a path to survival in a world where even minor mistakes were usually disastrous.

If there is any tragedy or evil in these rituals it is that the people who followed the examples of the early rituals failed to learn the appropriate lessons. After the holistic nature of ritual had been negated by the influence of technology, the rituals continued as barbarism in the name of ideology. The violence was continued without benefit of the holistic value of the ceremony. Men lost the community of the act and continued the savagery for the amusement of their ideological inclinations and dispositions.

Integration

The text has tried to establish the value of ritual inhumanity in effecting the integration of the individual into the ethnocentric community. Part of the important role of ritual in this endeavor was to recognize the individual, physically, spiritually and socially. The ordinary member of the community found his identity and his individuality through participation in the activities of the group. Individual self-perception in relationship to the group was reinforced by his personal acceptance of group values, norms and rituals. The actual physical participation gave him a sense of belonging, one that was reinforced by his sense of the spiritual community to which he belonged and the social acceptance that he came to experience. He owned a mark of acceptance, a mark that was his own and, at the same time, was a passport into the mysteries of community life. For the Arunta, this was a Churinga, or sacred stone, which each member received as a mark of his membership. For other initiates the mark was a scar or tattoo. Some kept the head of an enemy. But for each, in his own society, his token was a recognition device without which there was no admittance to the communal life.

When the community was small and tight knit the introduction of an individual into society was accompanied by the entire membership of the community. Public recognition was given to the entrance of a child and to the initiation of an adult. Often the young boy or girl was given a special name and status that gave the initiate a unique position in the tribe. The Arunta refrained from naming their children after deceased family. This provided a certain degree of originality and creativity in their culture. Inventing new names created new language and ways of thinking about things.

We have discussed other peoples who made special recognition of the child at birth and at puberty. Sometimes the father was required to go on a head hunting expedition in recognition of the importance of his new born infant. Other societies required bloodletting. Some cut off locks of hair. Often the child was made to surrender something of his own, this that he might be accepted as a member of the group. The prepuce of the male genital organ was an item commonly removed from the child. The ceremony of circumcision and the physical alteration in the male child was a common manner of establishing the special status of the neonate.

When the membership of the community was extensive the ritual was more selective. Individuals were noted not so much as members of the community. They were regarded as partisans of peculiar community segments. This segmentation and the consequent partial or selective recognition of the individual were functions of class structure. Class structure requires a social political development beyond the ethnocentric. The young Inca commoner was afforded a limited degree of recognition in ceremonial events. The Young Inca emperor, however, was given a good deal more attention and status. This approbation included the sacrifice of two hundred young children to the gods in his honor. The more complex the culture the more selective was the recognition. Status became a factor that followed the laws of social separation.

The simple recognition of the new member was not sufficient to secure his integration into the community. An initiation ceremony was necessary to assure his complete acceptance. Over a period of generations ritual became the only avenue to social membership and acceptance. Its importance in determining the initiation procedures for each person was paramount to the very process of integration. The initiation of each person into culture was to represent the fullest measure of his social and intellectual experience.

Chapter one discussed the process of integration in terms of a choice between membership and exclusion. The individual most often opted for inclusion in the group unless there was some mental or physical barrier to his entrance. A lame child or a mental defective, if they were to survive, would be social outcasts, not entitled to any of the regular benefits of community life. Occasionally there may have been a "wild bull" or "lone wolf" that chose not to accept the rules of the game and went off to live alone. There was also the special case of the shaman or witch doctor. But the ordinary imperative was for the tribesman to participate. From the moment of his birth, through his development and manhood he had been directed along those lines.

We have stated that there was a physical recognition of the initiate. There was also his physical involvement in the initiation, one that gave him an active and deliberate role to play. He was able, within limits, to determine his own social status. This was particularly the case in warrior societies. Among the Scythians a young man was required to kill an enemy, cut off his head and return with the trophy. His reward for this deed was to be allowed to drink the blood and wine mixture of the warrior ceremony. This made him a full-fledged member of the Scythian tribe. Indians of the Western Plains were required to mortify themselves for a period of time in order to be accepted as members of the tribe. The young novice was sometimes required to cut off flesh from his arms and legs. He might even cut off a finger joint. These rites gave the inductee a definitive, physical sense of belonging to the tribe. He had traded something of himself in exchange for the honor bestowed.

The point of this discussion, and the essay in general, is to demonstrate that this integration of the tribal member was very personal. It was not a group of boys or girls being recognized as a group. It was a group of boys or girls in which each member was recognized and accepted as an individual. There was no wholesale, assembly line introduction of members. Each individual had to prove his worth. Undoubtedly there were many instances in which an induction was postponed because the candidate was not ready. It is not unlikely that initiation was denied to misfits. This was to protect the integrity of the ceremony. This rejection insured the continuity and strength of the culture. Ethnocentric peoples are known to have been very particular about membership, paying close attention to those who were acceptable and those who were not. Initiation and membership were not automatic nor were they necessarily permanent. Credentials must be verified. Upon scrutiny they could be rescinded.

Among the most important effects of ritual upon the process of integration was the development of social solidarity. In our own day, there are those who are with us. There are those who are against us. This concept of "us against them" is not new to social science nor has it been under-researched. Konrad Lorenz called this phenomenon subspeciation and defined the attitude as a natural function of man's animal nature. It is from this concept that the notions of race and racial superiority are derived. Those who are not like us must be defective and therefore inferior. There have been enough holocausts in history to demonstrate that this concept of subspeciation was not an isolated ethnocentric prerogative.

Without the social tools to bypass this emotional reaction of subspeciation, learning, logic and empirical investigation, the idea was necessary to protect the continuity of the tribe. Ritual was designed to reinforce integration in a specific culture and in a specific group. Outsiders were automatically excluded. One recalls the practice of the Ganda when their king died. Strangers were killed. Those who were "alien" were strangled. This bound together those who "belonged." There is a certain measure of xenophobia in this practice although the sense of social solidarity was not predicated upon a fear of outsiders as much as distaste for their alien status. The Cheyenne referred only to themselves as human beings. The remainder of mankind was thought to be something just a little inferior. The Jew calls the rest of mankind gentiles. The Romans referred to everyone non-roman as a barbarian. The Greeks and the Chinese kept a similar attitude.

Because of the very thin line between survival and extinction many of the tribes discussed in the text are shown to have had an intense attachment to this sense of social solidarity. The ritual that reinforced that solidarity was equally important. Consider the impetus given to the Hindu farmer when he acquired a piece of human flesh to bury in his soil. This was his offering to Kali. Consider the sense of community and surety that he must have felt by his participation in this ceremony. The ritual provided him with the flesh that, he believed, was going to insure his crop. These rituals might seem barbaric but they had their purposes. The more gruesome they were the greater the purpose they seemed to serve. The sense of belonging that came from the first battle trophy or the first cup of the enemy's blood to drink was very often the "glue" that held very simple societies together. Even more complex societies, such as the Phoenicians, needed an occasional sacrifice to Marduk or Tanit in order to draw the people together, especially in times of crisis.

The danger in this intense feeling of solidarity was that the identity of the individual was lost in the holistic expression of the group. His own proclivities and aspirations were nullified by a kind of "howling mob" unity that seems to have plagued the human community throughout the centuries. The danger of the individual losing his identity in the mob is quite real. The danger of losing identity in anarchy is also present creating a serious threat to the facade of culture. Where there is no cultural bond between people there can be no realistic personal identity because there can be no reference for that identity. Integration through ritual is truly the lifeblood of cultural development.

The logical consequence of this holistic communal attitude is the recognition of a social purpose and mission. Ritual played a major role in missionary activities within cultures because it was often the sole means of educating the young. Many of the tasks that were set before an initiate were designed to be instructive as well as inductive. The Aztec child had to learn about the value of pain and self-torture so that, by his own performance, he might please the gods and insure the continuity of Aztec civilization. In war he must learn that live captives were for the gods. His human efforts would insure that the sun might keep itself in the sky. His sense of social purpose was reinforced by the need for his own spiritual and, as the Aztecs believed, physical survival. The aristocrats of the Shang dynasty had a similar purpose when they used their captives to mollify the ancestors and the gods.

The point of ritual, as it applies to social mission, is to insure that the community survives. The clan can only survive if the young are instructed properly. Ritual taught them their duties to their elders and to society. This is as true for the modern man as it was for the ethnocentric man. Warrior communities must impress upon their adherents the value of war, hunting and physical aggression. Agricultural communities must pass on their knowledge of the seasons and the arts of growing crops to future generations to insure the success of the farming community. The transmission of knowledge must be emphatic to insure acceptance. Part of the explanation for the violence of ritual in many communities was their need to emphasize the importance of the subject being taught.

As it was practiced among the Hindus and the Sumerians, suttee was a function of integration. The rite had community approval and participation. In many cases suttee was simply an expression of autocracy which showed no regard for individual identity. Often it served to recognize, initiate and accept an individual into his society. Despite the inevitable consequence, the person was both the envy and the admiration of his fellow citizens. Devotion to a leader, which made necessary following him in death, obviously gave one a sense of social mission as well as an acute sense of belonging to a select group. Where full community participation was elicited by the ceremony the function of integration was well served.

Human sacrifice, like suttee, was a public spectacle. Individual members found an object of communal endeavor and support in the victim. The victim was an object upon which all the emotional feeling of the populace could be discharged. Certain feelings and hatred could not be discharged by one individual upon another because of social taboos. The public sacrifice was a vicarious replacement for this discharge. It is no wonder that the victim was sometimes torn to shreds by the howling mob. Human sacrifice also provided many of the physical "trophies" which served as instruments of socialization.

Ornaments provide one of the best examples of ritual and its integrative value. In our own society we have many reifying objects. These serve to draw our attention to ourselves as a special people. Not the least of these is a flag. In ethnocentric societies the "flags" were more gruesome but just as effective in introducing the individual to his culture. Scalps, heads and other appendages were ample evidence of a person's acceptance and position in society.

Cultural Selection

We have averred that ritual was an expedient of social integration that created a sense of social purpose and mission. Under the heading of cultural selection ritual will be considered as a measure of social control. The selection of specific rituals was made according to the need for control and the most appropriate manner of control. Aztecs, for example, were a small minority in a larger Meso-American population. Still they managed to conquer and dominate the greater part of this population. The reason was the Aztec penchant for barbarity. They were thoroughly conditioned to the practice of savage rites. The atrocities that they inflicted upon other peoples were not even as intense as were those that they practiced upon themselves. Culturally, they opted for self-torture and asceticism. The spiritual toughness that derived from self-affliction was imperative to their survival as a "Master" race. Their self-control was brought about by the practice of ritual, which was, in turn, a measure of cultural selection.

The same might be said of the austere Plains Indians who used self-inflicted misery to seek truth, wisdom and strength. These visionaries struggled for self control in order to survive a harsh and merciless climate. The young Cheyenne warrior who bled himself and cut off one of his finger joints was looking for more that just a vision. In his manhood rite he was trying to find the will and strength to survive.

Any form of intentional social conditioning is designed to impose controls. Ritual anticipates self-control. Not every person will voluntarily punish himself for his transgressions or obey the law of his own accord. Without social guidance man is more apt to respond to nature than to culture. Culture is often the antithesis of nature. The imposition of ritual was designed to channel individual activity into more or less rigid and structured patterns of behavior. This is evident in our own literate societies. We teach children to read so they can read whatever we want them to read. We teach them to pray so that they can recite "our" prayers. Ethnocentric peoples imposed selective rituals upon their members to achieve the same ends. Members must account for their attitudes and actions. Where the ritual was public the imposition of control was stronger and enduring.

In primitive societies there was a time and place for everything. Ritual determined the regularity of life. Upon rising, a person said his prayers, ate his food, dressed himself and then aspired to some social goal or daily task. Ritual guided all of these activities. Social control of this kind assured the consistency of life. At times such rites many have been harsh. They were also indispensable to the integration of the individual. Ritual limited activity within the social sphere creating patterns that allowed social harmony and community well being.

The need for social control was not the only factor that determined the selection of behavioral options. There were also ecological or environmental factors. As social necessity required a controlling ritual ecology often defined its practice. Geography was an important element in determining the attitudes of primitives toward both life and ritual. In the forest ritual was not the same as it was in the desert. One might say that each of the different climatic regions of the world developed its own special reactions to existence. In the desert, where the sun is constant and environmental factors relatively constant, there were few gods in the local pantheon. In the forest, where shadows, noises and streams of water were frequent and varied, there were many and diverse gods. It is interesting to note that the concept of one god came from a people who originated in the hot dry desert. Naturally the number and choices of rituals varied with the number of available deities.

Environmental factors determined the manner in which people earned their livelihood. Water peoples practiced water rituals to insure continued economic fortune. Agricultural peoples conducted fertility rituals to enhance the productivity of the soil. Forest peoples developed hunting rites. These climatic circumstances and economic pursuits created different kinds of ritual inhumanity. The Tang, who relied upon the river, threw young virgins into the streams to appease the water gods. The Celts, who lived in the forests, made offerings to their gods in a separate fashion. They hung victims from the trees that abounded in the forests. The Great World Ash, the tree of Oden, headed the Celtic pantheon. The Hindus and the Pawnee Indians dissected their corn maidens and buried them in the earth. The list is endless and its recitation would be tiring. Suffice it to say that the ecology of a group was one of the main factors in determining its own ritual brand. This fact adds some sense to the apparently meaningless barbarity of many of these practices.

Generally speaking, the developments of suttee, human sacrifice and the use of ornaments were related, ritually, to the ecological factor. All of these practices reflect a concern for the cycles of nature and for the constancy of birth, death and rebirth. Head hunting and cannibalism also reflected an intimacy with nature. These two were more pronounced in the most primitive peoples. The forced burial of individuals in the earth alongside their leaders, a planting which was expected to yield an eternal crop, was not characteristic of any group to the exclusion of any other. The practice did find its most refined expression among the early agricultural civilizations. Where the ecological factor favored the extensive development of agriculture this ritual seems to have been more evident. The use of human sacrifice in rituals of rebirth was more restricted. Among the forest peoples the rite was more often a votive offering to a celestial deity than to a terrestrial one. That is to say that the Earth Mother and her appetite did not figure prominently outside of the agricultural sphere. The relationship between head hunting, cannibalism and rebirth and the cycles of nature should, by now, be obvious.

Personal factors also mattered. The style in which individuals respond to given cultural stimuli varies with that elusive element called the human factor. What is acceptable to one generation is often repugnant to the next. Others may scorn what one or more individuals readily embrace. This phenomenon makes cultural selection an important feature in the growth of group personality. The environment remains relatively constant through one generation. If it does change, the change is usually slow enough that it is not really noticed. The need for social stability and social control are also constant. Personalities, however, are too complex to be entirely predictable. The selection of ritual can alter the psychological composition of society and its mission.

In some societies the development of ritual has proceeded toward an accommodation of different personalities and social dispositions. These rituals were designed primarily for men. Women were also given certain behavioral options with which to develop their own attitudes and feelings. Among the Indians of North America there were a number of tribes who kept what one might properly call a "men's" club. Many of these sub-cultural units were oriented toward the warriors. Obviously these groups were arranged to allow for the venting of hostile emotions in a socially acceptable way. We have already discussed the advantages of the headhunting raid in this respect. Some of these warrior cults even contained an inner group for those who were especially ferocious.

The Cheyenne Indians had a warrior group called the Contraries. These young men did everything backward in relation to what one would ordinarily expect. If they were leaving they would walk backwards as though they might be approaching. This departure was accompanied by the word for hello instead of that for goodbye. The warriors were usually quite young and dedicated themselves strictly to war and violence.

Another group, among the Kwakiutl Indians, was called the Cannibal Society. Members were selected from the general population. They were chosen for their great daring and bravery. The successful candidates became devotees of a god called the Cannibal who lived at the North End of the World. These cannibals were similar to the Contraries. They were the most violent and uncompromising of the group. Their deity was a god of carnage, bloodshed and violence. It was believed that the god Cannibal devoured his victims all at one time. Initiation rites, which encouraged the savage personality, included the ritual eating of human flesh. Among these Indians, the Cannibals were at the top of the social ladder. Membership was often determined by birthright as though the violence was hereditary. The violent personality, properly oriented, was the goal of those who sought the esteem of their fellows.

The Vikings had a special kind of warrior called a Berserk. This man was contumaciously violent. His entire purpose was to charge into battle, in a fit of rage, and hack to pieces any enemy that he might encounter. It was the Berserk, and his totally irrational behavior, that made the Norsemen feared throughout Europe. The only apparent qualification for this title was a personality disposed to violence. Like the Cannibals and the Contraries, the Berserk lived at the apex of Viking society. He was revered as a hero.

Naturally, each of these groups had its own rituals. To achieve the desired effect, the rites were developed and performed to reinforce patterns of violence and personality. One might see in its rituals an attempt by society to control the spontaneous use of violence. Proper channels were provided through which hostile emotions could be dispelled. Ethnocentrics must have realized and made provision for those of their members who were uncontrollably violent. The selection of specific rituals to channel that violence was an important factor in social control as well.

The same provisions were often made for those whose personalities seemed truly erratic though not necessarily violent. There were those who had emotional or physical disorders such as epilepsy, fits or mental retardation. These were sometimes given a special social status. The shaman in most societies was usually a person who had an extremely mercurial and yet withdrawn personality. As shamans were believed to go into trances in order to send their spirits into other worlds, a moody and inward disposition was most certainly an asset. The advantage, however, could backfire. If there were times of great hardship or unrest the shaman could be in danger. Those who seemed, by their introverted personalities, to be set apart, were often used as scapegoats. Many were murdered without having a chance to defend themselves.

Much has been written about the way in which individuals react to their society and how society molds individuals to its own standards. The two great anthropologists, Margaret Mead and Ruth Benedict, took both sides of this issue in their studies and examined them thoroughly. Whether the individual or society had the greatest influence, the fact is that the interaction of different types of personalities profoundly affected the development and expression of ritual in ethnocentric societies. Personal, ecological and social factors worked to make small, imperceptible, but significant changes in the practice of ritual inhumanity. Man has always been a creatively adaptive creature. He makes small adjustments to changes in his situations. Many of these changes are brought forth from his technological innovations. New cultural developments required the institution of new rituals in order to reestablish social harmony that had been disrupted by change.

Sometimes these changes were a combination of technological innovation and nature. One common example is the domestication of the horse. The domestication of this animal brought forth a tremendous mobility. Pastoral, agricultural people were suddenly catapulted into the world of the nomadic warrior. The consequent concentration on hunting, the development of the tools of war and the introduction of military strategies altered social attitudes radically. These altered attitudes, coupled with the ability to conquer and destroy, led to the increase of barbarism and ritual inhumanity. The Scythians were such a people. They adapted the horse to their culture and turned into a wandering horde of warriors who ravaged other lands.

A more radical example was that of the Cheyenne who made the same transition. The Scythians required centuries to develop their nomadic life. The Cheyenne managed to accomplish the same feat in less than fifty years. They changed from a predominantly agricultural, corn growing civilization into a nomadic, warrior group who hunted buffalo. This happened in less than two generations. It is interesting to note that the Cheyenne society did not survive the transition. The increased mobility brought the Indians into direct conflict with the

U.S. Cavalry. In contrast, the Hopi Indians, who did not develop the use of the horse, survived the onslaught of the white man and continue to this day.

Another obvious instance of the effects of change is the exchange or borrowing of customs. Sometimes one group imposed customs upon another. Only the remotest areas of the world have escaped the effects of cultural diffusion. Many changes were brought about by the collision of ideas and ritual practices. This occurred to such a degree in some areas that one generation's ritual practices might have little or no relation to that of its parent. The areas of the world, such as Sumeria, which have been the crossroads of diverse military peoples seem to have been the ones affected the most.

The effects could be severe and sometimes culturally destructive. The Celts, for example, were known for their Furor Teutonicus. In the space of a generation they were conquered and ruled by Roman administrators. Gerhard Herm says that they almost immediately lost their ferocity and their zest for war and killing. The Roman Legions had destroyed the lifeblood of their cultural bond. The same was true of the Solomon Islanders who endured the dictates of British Colonial Policy. When the ban on head hunting was imposed the cultural life of the community seemed to fade until it actually ceased to exist. The stories of the effects of colonial administration around the world are similar.

Impermanence

Man has been in collusion and collision with his environment throughout his history. At the same time he has been an integral part of the natural cycle. He has remained a wholly separate and synergistic expression of evolutionary development. He is a species beyond the pale of natural continence and contiguity. Unlike any other creature, he keeps an awareness of the impermanence attached to himself and the world around him. Armed with this burdensome knowledge, he has tried in diverse ways to fortify himself against the vicissitudes of fortune. Ritual is a logical and necessary consequence of this attempt to deal with the changes in life. It is through ritual that one strives to challenge the problems of change and death.

Heraclitus said that no man could put his foot into the same stream twice. However slight the effort and however brief the instance of immersion time has altered the composition of the stream and the foot. Nature does not exist in a state of being. Nature exists in a state of becoming. Ethnocentrics had no wherewithal to challenge this concept philosophically. They accepted the notion of change as an environmental constant. Change was a factor to be observed and manipulated. In their own energetic and demonstrative manner they tried to establish control over this impermanence. Frazer has suggested that primitive peoples, through the use of homeopathic and contiguous magic, executed this attempt. The essence of the argument is that man tried to control his environment by ritual. He tried to duplicate the appearance of nature. A corn ritual anticipated a bountiful corn harvest. A war dance before battle anticipated victory over the enemy. Wounds inflicted on him or others before battle were supposed to insure that the warriors, having already been wounded, would escape harm in battle. Frazer discussed the many and elaborate ways in which these primitives tried to preclude the disastrous effects of change.

The view that one could affect the course of natural events through the use of sympathetic magic is a very solipsistic one. However, the development of ritual was generated from that principle of narcissism. Man tried to provide himself with a sense of control. The pattern continues to the present day. The modern person who wears a cross or a rabbit foot for luck is little different, in intention, from the more distant ancestor who wore a scalp on his belt as a sign of power over his enemies. The aim was to compete with, confound and overcome the laws of chance. The notion, which avers the relationship between the control of nature and change and the use of contiguous magic, is a very human one. The centuries have not dulled the sensitivity of man to his own need for a pretended immutability. He lives, after all, in a world of constant flux.

The development of ritual was similar to the development of man. The process reflects a synergistic expression of its inherent parts. As change occurred ritual changed. This caused a further social change. Change and ritual became interdependent. We have already discussed the effects of change on society. Ordinarily there is a balance that is maintained between regularity and flux. Change is accepted as a potent force in the development of ritual. There are things that are apparently immutable and things that are in a constant state of alteration. Ritual was, and is, the social means through which problems are made reasonable and acceptable to those who are most affected by their occurrence. The state of equilibrium in society, which is constantly being adjusted, is acceptable to the group and the individual if the balance perceived can be controlled by ritual action. As long as man has a sense of his power, through ritual, over the confrontations he makes, then he is satisfied with the constant change.

In the social history of mankind death has always been recognized as the great equalizer. Death recognizes no boundaries of social or political design. It spares no person by rank or social station. Death is the ineluctable consequence of life. One's passing is the greatest and most profound confrontation that the human spirit must experience. That great enemy, whose incidence is callously indifferent to human timetables and plans, was first challenged by the development of ritual.

The problem of change and the problem of death were first challenged by a solipsistic attitude. Man convinced himself that he had control over the Grim Reaper. The least advanced societies accomplished this by ascribing to each particle of nature the quality of life. Trees, rocks, sand, grass, plants, animals and people were all alive. The advent of death was a simple transition from one life form to another. The concept was reinforced by the practice of ritual inhumanity. In fact, death was brought about deliberately to insure a proper transition!

In a ritual designed to reenact the cycles of nature, the body of an individual was sometimes cut up and buried in the earth. This kind of rite was usually associated with a fertility ceremony. The early Greek field festivals offered human sacrifice to the Great Goddess. The Aztec priests killed thousands of war captives every year. They believed this action would keep the sun in the sky and insure the continuity of day and night. The Hindus offered the youngest and fairest of the Meriah to be torn to pieces by the mob. Each piece of human flesh was then buried in the fields. For the observers of these rituals these actions reinforced the notion that death was a necessary part of life. Death was an exigent process in the cycles of nature. The tiniest being could make its proper transition at the proper place and time. Whatever barbaric ritual was employed its purpose was to reaffirm that there was no separation between man and his environment. The affront of death was overcome by simply making death a phase of life.

The more advanced civilizations recognized that this holistic view of life was not entirely correct. They saw that it was not philosophically practical. Their solution was to create a greater separation between man and the elements. This solution was sufficient to preclude a serious attachment to the idea that simple being was not equitable with the life process. More careful thinkers suggested that death actually upset the balance of life in the universe. That is to say that all beings do not have life and do not participate in the struggle for existence. The reaction of early civilizations to this concept of separation was a series of provisions for a separate, nether world, into which a man's spirit, now divested of his earthly appurtenances, would pass.

The Egyptians developed the process of embalming which they used in the mummification of bodies. For more important members of the community they constructed a necropolis, or city of the dead. Mummified corpses of the elite, and a few select retainers, were believed to carry on as they had in their earthly life. In the early mastabas, which were pre-pyramid burial pits, servants and wives were killed and then buried with their departed masters. Chapter two discussed in some detail the similar practices among the Sumerians, Thracians, Chinese, Vikings and Scythians. These all represent efforts on the part of more advanced civilizations to overcome death by making death a transition to another form of life. It was such an attempt, at least, on the part of the elite in those societies. This is not the same as saying that the people who practiced suttee among these more advanced cultures were attempting to return to nature. They did not believe in the Hindu concept. They were decidedly opposed to that concept. They fully intended to keep their own bodies, their own possessions and their own personalities. In these growing cultures there had been a definitive advance away from the concept of total reliance upon the Great Earth Goddess.

There were other, more immediate attempts, to deal with death. The offering of human beings in sacrifice during times of war, famine and epidemic was common among many peoples. Often the idea was to prolong one's life by trading that of another. This was not a particularly altruistic sentiment. Certainly it was a human one. The Aztecs were probably the most notorious for human sacrifice. The Hindus were nearly as prolific in their efforts. The Hindu goddess Kali had to be "fed." Once fed the deity would function properly and assure security and longevity to those who had accomplished the feeding. This is an obvious example of Man's belief in his role as a key player in the very existence of nature. If the gods were not cared for they would wither away and nature would follow them. It is the very human and solipsistic attitude that is so fundamental to the preservation of ritual and ritual inhumanity. In the practice lies the justification for the most heinous act of man, his desire to insure the continuity of nature and the future of the species.

One obvious aspect of impermanence and the problem of death is the challenge to the will and power of man. The challenge was one that could not be refused. Perhaps the greatest philosophical accomplishment of humanity is the acceptance of that challenge. It is difficult to assess this accomplishment because it represents the peculiar quality of man that indeed separates him from the rest of nature.

Part of the explanation of this phenomenon is to be found in the intellectual definition of man. Here is a creative creature that lives most of his life in what psychologists call the cognitive domain. Man is a cognitive, reasoning being who, given the resources and the opportunity, can produce the technology to solve the simplest or the most complex of problems. In the course of its existence no other being can do that same thing as well as man. Here is a being that could develop agriculture from his observation of plant life. He could manufacture implements of peace and war. To some degree man could control the very forces of nature. Yet for all his sophistication and technological potential he could not, do very much about the inevitability of dying. The affront to that great intellectual, technological human personality must have been as powerfully ego rending fifty thousand years ago as it is today. It is little wonder that the rituals surrounding death were so complex and so attentive to the least detail. Man and his rituals had to hide the fact that empirical science alone could not, even through trial and error, overcome the Grim Reaper.

It is to his credit as an ingenious thinker and as a dauntless spirit that man accepted the challenge of impermanence. He has developed countless cultural complexities that extend well beyond the potential of natural evolution. In the uses of magic and religion he has tried to overcome the most difficult metaphysical barriers. His acceptance of the challenge has meant that his progress is always in motion. That movement has carried him further and further away from the earth that gave him life and supported him, physically and spiritually, in the dark hours of his cultural infancy.

His ritual has reflected the practical aspects of everyday life. This has moved man away from the cycles of nature. He has progressed from a belief in the Great Earth Goddess to a belief in gods who dwell beyond the stars; the very stars that he can see but cannot reach. I am not suggesting here that God is simply the unknown or the unreachable. Through the course of religious development He has always seemed to be beyond the reach of the immediate physical reality. We cling tenaciously to our own physical reality and that reality is the place where we expect to find God. Somewhere during this process toward the heavens man has fashioned the notion that the progression toward the Ouranic has made him a more sophisticated and cultured creature. Despite this newfound cultural elegance human sacrifice continued. This time the offering was made to the sun god or sky god instead of the Great Mother. Human trophies, such as heads and other body parts, were still acceptable in the worship of celestial beings. Despite the alterations in ritual and the reasons for the practice, ritual inhumanity was fairly consistent. One might expect this. After all, pain and suffering and barbarism are sense oriented. Ritual was certainly designed to appeal to the senses.

In the process of cultural development, despite the continuity of inhumane acts, ritual inhumanity was gradually losing its value. Over time the processes that had been seriously engaged for their integrative value became more and more a source of amusement. The practices became increasingly specialized and less responsive to the holistic expression of the community. In the movement away from nature there was a redefinition of social values and socially acceptable behavior. These changes precluded a serious expression of the holistic. Eventually the practices were reduced to sport.

The Transition to Segmentation

Given the very nature of cultural development it is obvious that the holistic, simplex community could not long continue except as a specialized part of a larger social group. The interactions between separate, previously isolated societies led to changes that allowed for more complex social incorporation. The economic, social and political divisions of the larger state precluded a return to the pastoral life. The transition to segmentation was the beginning of this social separation and stratification.

The how and why of this social separation is perhaps not as important as its consequences. Maybe one group conquered another and divided the labor of the tribe among the vanquished. This set up the first division of labor. Perhaps the division of labor was along sexual or religious lines for another group. As smaller groups incorporated themselves into larger ones the origins vanished in the complexity of the transition to the socially stratified community. The point is that there was a marked progression toward social separation generated by the interaction and mixing of separate communities. This stratification naturally initiated and sustained a number of social inequalities through which a class or caste system developed.

Many of these systems were feudal or monarchical in nature. They were based upon a certain kind of exploitation of labor in which individuals vied for power and wealth through the efforts of others who were restrained from so competing by their social station. This is not a Marxian critique of social development. It is apparent that the start of social separation made necessary the fact that some individuals control the economic structure. To be viable a community must be a profitable enterprise. That entails leadership and social stratification. It was in this separation of peoples that a certain class structure developed. Segmentation facilitated the social development of the group at the same time that it radically modified its ritual development. Not every group in society came to subscribe to or to be controlled by the same ritual.

In an extremely isolated group every member of the community was intimately familiar with every other member. This included their activities, personalities and dispositions. Within such a group the learning process was very straightforward. It required little modification and a considerable measure of mnemonic repetition. In less remote circumstances the tribal solidarity might be more relaxed. There were clans, moieties and social clubs. These precluded some membership based upon heredity, social position, military prowess or physical appearance. Among many Indian tribes of North America men's clubs were based on birth or some other qualifying factor. We have already discussed this phenomenon among the cannibals of the Northwest Indians. There were also bear clubs, lion clubs and wolf clubs. Perhaps any animal of note might be so employed by the tribe to formulate an inner group. The point is that there was a separation of status based upon subscription to a certain animal cult. So men of the same tribe might be divided along lines of "party" membership. They were ideologically separated.

The ideological aspirations of primitives were somewhat limited by geopolitical and technological circumstances. In more advanced societies, such as China, there were ideological differences expressed by differences in class and status. In China were the don and the peon, the servant and master. Each knew his place and kept it well. Here there were intrigues of gothic proportions in which one faction plotted against another. The history of such monarchies is speckled with the accounts of petty intrigues. One faction or another sought for the favor of the crown or the crown itself. John Bergamini's book, The Tragic Dynasty, a History of the Romanovs is a delightful exposition of such triumphs and failures.

It should be noted that ideology among primitives is not the same and was not understood as it might be today. There were no closely defined dogmas to be preached to the faithful. There was a sense of separateness. This led people to consider themselves as part of segments of society rather than as integrants in a holistic group. Ideology was a new and disruptive element in the cultural experience of humans. Ideology made much of diversity and rather little of sameness. The individual found his identity with the group. He was beginning to lose the holistic consciousness of an integrated member. Membership in a special group did more to reinforce his ego. The social separations that were engendered by the stratification of society, for whatever reason, could only be affected by the development of government. The feudal and monarchical nature of early civilizations tended to reinforce the segmentation of individuals. The result was a decided division between the ordinary folk and the ruling folk, between society and the state.

Among some tribes this separation was intended to protect the monarch. He was considered responsible for the well being of the community. As long as the king was in good condition the rest of society would fare well. According to Frazer, this resulted in an inordinate number of taboos. These restrictions were placed upon both the people and the king. In some communities people were not allowed to watch the king drink or eat. The fear was that such a vision would upset the balance of nature. But these restrictions soon gave way to greedier designs. Those who were close to the king might be able to control him and to make themselves the masters of the community. The ultimate master was he who could most cleverly manipulate the rituals. The possibility of factionalism and the advent of ideology are evident in the efforts of those who would control the throne without actually being king.

The intent of all this discussion is to demonstrate that ideology created a new order and made easier the manipulation of various segments of society. Technology and socioeconomic development enhanced the social structure and facilitated the separation of community and government that in turn spurred the growth of ideology.

A final aspect of segmentation was the development of the secular world. Various scholars have discussed the roles of religion and magic in the cultural growth of communities. Some say that magic is a degenerative form of religion while others maintain that religion is a logical extension of magic. Certainly the development of ritual and of inhumanity relied upon these factors heavily. At least this was true in the early phases of cultural experience. No headhunter would readily admit that his war trophies had no spiritual power. No shaman would suggest that the human bones with which he augured events were worthless spiritually. No Indian warrior would believe that the scalps on his war shirt were simply decorations. All of these items, and countless others, were believed to hold power. The owner could use this power either against his enemies or on behalf of his loved ones. As James Frazer has suggested, the savage world relied upon a belief in its ability to manipulate the world.

But the world of this so-called savage was not a secular one. There was little opportunity for more than a few individuals to escape from the confines of group ritual. They were all bound to either their religion or their magic. Perhaps the social pariahs and the shamans could egress from the complexity of rituals. The ordinary citizen was tied to the ceremonies for the length and benefit of his life. The old wild bull, living alone in the woods, scorned by the company of his fellows, might make light of the social niceties. But in primitive existence the stalwart citizens of the tribal community could ill afford to abuse the sacred traditions of their forbears. Disaster might ensue.

The synergistic quality of technology made the secular world possible. Through the propitious use of material resources some societies developed a better standard of living. This allowed considerable leisure for part of the citizenry. The Greeks had this advantage in their golden age. In that time they developed the marvelous philosophies which still echo through the millenniums. The Romans, a less philosophical people, put their ingenuity to work to develop a practical economy that relied upon the prowess of Roman engineers and military strategists. There was more influence of the Forum and less of Capitoline Jupiter and priests. These examples are not intended to suggest that one civilization or another had a monopoly upon secular activities. They could definitely not sustain a consistent development of society separate from the religious and magical world. The fall of both Greece and Rome amply demonstrate that the factors are too complex for such a simple view. They are rather intended to demonstrate that the gradual development of technological expertise facilitated the movement away from the magic-religion connection toward the practical scientific view of life.

No evolutionary development, physical, spiritual or technological follows a straight line toward the "truth." There are progressions, regressions and long periods of stasis. All of these interlace within the movement toward a more technologically sophisticated world. Not all members of society experience the intellectual impact of these evolutionary trends. In the modern world people still believe in witches, demons and magic. In accord with the fears and superstitions that are generated by these beliefs the practice of ritual inhumanity continues among modern men. The movement toward the secular erased the primary function of ritual inhumanity and replaced that function with an ideological inhumanity. It is in this erasure, however slight and subtle, that the transmission to a segmented society began.

# *Epilogue*

Et ecce equus pallidus; et, qui sedebat desuper,
nomen illi Mors, et Infernus sequbatur eum...
Apocalypsis Ioannis

6:8
Novum Testamentum Latine

"And behold a pale horse; and, he who sat upon
him, was named Death, and Hell followed him"
**Revelations**

**6:8**

**Latin New Testament**

# Afterword

Some of the scholars who have studied the Nazi Holocaust have suggested that the impetus for this dreadful chapter in history be predicated upon a cultural conflict between Germans and Jews. The Germans, it is argued, were a "Volk" or people who were looking for a way to reestablish the holistic community that they believed had existed in past times. This community could be restored. They were interested in culture, community and ritual that would bring them closer to their "German nature" The Jews, on the other hand, were said to be without culture and only interested in science, technology and money.

The resulting conflict became one of war between religion and science, between traditional values and modernity, between the holistic and the disparate. It is argued that the Jews were "purged" from German society to "protect" the purity of German blood and culture and to reestablish a holistic German culture and people. The worst atrocities of the Aztecs and the Carthaginians, in which they sacrificed thousands of captives to their respective gods, pale in comparison to the gas chambers and crematories of the Third Reich. Yet there is a certain common theme in the execution of both sacrificial processes.

There is the individual and there is the group, the need for personal liberty and the need for group cohesion. Ritual was and is an avenue toward both. But ritual has its limit when it begins to crush personal liberty under the weight of oppression and the threat of racial annihilation. In his book, Life Unworthy of Life, James Glass described the idea that there is no moral or ethical value that can transcend the power of the state. Ultimately the power of the state will overcome the individual. Certainly this has been true among those governments that we call totalitarian.

It is important to study the history of ritual in order that we may learn the true nature and possibilities of horrendous acts such as human sacrifice. Certainly the modern centuries have provided clear-cut examples of such violence. The modern authoritarian penchant for "Ethnic cleansing" seems alive and well in our days. Often it is coupled with some religious fervor that adds oil to the fire. The conflict in Kosovo was only one in a long string of such sad cases.

Let us all learn from our primitive forbears about the nature of ritual and the limit of its uses that we do not fall prey to the temptation of holocaust violence. As men and women we have come from the shadows of antiquity into the light of modern knowledge and understanding. Let us not ignore or extinguish the light in favor of the perdition that lies, ever watchful, in the darkness.

# Conclusions

There is a need for ritual. The first chapter of this book described the need of the individual to find some sort of personal identity. That identity was to be found through his interaction with others. He became a person by establishing, through his participation in ritual, a relationship with the rest of his kind. Despite the changes which have ensued during the countless millennia in which man has been on this planet that need remains. The psychologists say that the individual needs to belong. The sociologist and the anthropologist would concur. In fact, there is no branch of modern behavioral science that would suggest that the individual would function optimally without the presence of others of his species. It is this sense of belonging that reinforces the need for ritual, the need for some mechanism whereby the continuity of existence can be sustained. The individual must have some assurance that he will find meaning and substance in his life. In the course of human social development it has always been ritual that has provided this assurance. It seems unlikely that there is any better mechanism whereby that assurance can be guaranteed.

The need for ritual is obviously reflected in the growth of segmentation in the modern world. Very often, within modern industrial states, there is a separation of individuals into ideological camps. The existence of these separate ideological components very often hinders good cultural health. In some countries these factions are capable, in a single political move, of completely changing the form of government. In other more democratic communities factionalism tends to suppress certain groups such that they experience intense social distress. The holistic communal experience is so diminished that people have killed one another wantonly just to reinforce their own beliefs. The manner in which US Seventh Cavalry responded to the "Indian threat" in the

179

last century is a typical example. A more recent instance was the Nazi holocaust in Eastern Europe in which the complete segmentation of a group on one side led to the complete segmentation and destruction of a group on the other side. The racial measures of the Ku Klux Klan reflect their own horror stories. There were atrocities committed in the name of ideology. The 1917 Bolsheviks, though more egalitarian in the application of their ideological policies, were on a par with the others. It has been estimated, for example that Joseph Stalin, in his long reign, was responsible for the liquidation of fifty million people. All of this was done in the name of ideology. Among modern men, these examples are the most notorious and far outweigh any barbarism committed by their primitive antecedents in the name of communal solidarity. But they aptly demonstrate the consequences of segmentation in the modern world. How many civil wars in how many different lands, where father killed son and brother butchered brother, were brought into being in the name of Ideology?

I am not suggesting that ideologies have no value or place in the modern world. In fact, ideology is important to social progress because it is, and always has been, a precipitator of change. In the cultural development of human beings change is the most critical factor. But change, which often comes fast and furious, is not always socially healthy. The value of tradition and ritual, even in these sophisticated times, is in its ability to moderate viewpoints and the changes which opinion and belief engender. Some attention must be paid to ritual so that innovation can be a creative and constructive asset to any community rather than a radical and debilitating liability. The cultural experience of ritual can limit the deleterious consequence of social segmentation.

A final peril with which modern societies are faced is one that seems to be expressed more often in these quickly changing times. That is the danger of alienation. In a primitive, integrated society it was not usually possible for an individual to be outside his group socially and still survive. People relied too heavily upon one another for their very survival. In a society in which the initial phases of ideological development are beginning to appear, dissatisfaction is usually resolved by attachment to a specific group which, by its policy, defines or redefines the individual's social role. Very often the success of an ideological movement depends upon its ability to satisfy the social needs of its adherents. In that case alienation is discarded in favor of a new social role. The danger here is that the person is not likely to consider the ethical value of his participation because his need for acceptance has overshadowed his sense of judgment. This is the case with many obviously good people who joined the Nazi Party. In a society in which the cultural development has extended beyond ideological factions, such as in our own post-industrial society, the individual is forgotten in a maze of technological litter. I once had a sociology professor whose greatest fear was that everyone in America would have his own audio video system and would be relieved of the need to communicate with any of his fellow humans. That is a nightmare that looms imminently.

The periodicals that report the news and opinion of the modern world are sprinkled with accounts of individuals who have committed bizarre and heinous acts against humanity. There have been numerous copies of the original Jack the Ripper. The Boston Strangler, Lizzie Borden, the Zodiac Killer and many others have all demonstrated an acute anti-social behavior. That is their common denominator. They all lost touch with the social order. A feeling of community and a sense of purpose were missing. In a sense they created their own inhumane rituals to satisfy that need. The great danger of alienation is that it fosters this persistent expression of dissatisfaction with the community. For the alienated, the ordinary processes of social development and expression are lacking. By that lack of social expression the extremes of anti social behavior are encouraged. How sad a world it would be if each individual on this planet felt the same alienation.

The late French priest, Pierre Tielhard de Chardin wrote a book in the 1950's called The Phenomenon of Man. When I first looked at the volume I was only seventeen. Sixteen years passed before I actually read the book in its entirety. Now some forty years have passed since that first perusal. There is no other volume of literature on the subject of mankind that has had more influence upon this writing than that slim, intense and informative book by Father Chardin. In his essay on man he called for a return to the holistic in the modern world. With him I also wish to call for a return to the holistic.

Chardin viewed the development of nature as a process in which complexity is developed through the synthesis of individuals in nature and the very process of their development. Through the natural process there is an ever growing and ever convoluting complexity. For Chardin man is at the apex of that process and is the end result of nature's effort. But man remains in a constant state of change, ever increasing the intensity and complexity of his being.

The old biological saw that ontogeny recapitulates phylogeny applies to his view of the world. Man's development is a microcosm of nature's broader development. Man takes his growth one step further than nature in that he can create a psychosocial process. His social institutions can continue this convolution well beyond whatever nature might achieve on its own. Man, therefore, can create a holistic world in which all of his best features, physical and psychic, can by congealed to accelerate this "Complexification." At the same time he can retain that individual nature which creates the "mutant" alterations in him that caused the changes to occur in the first place.

The question here remains one of choices. How does one determine if an individual input into the holistic convolution is benign or malignant? To what degree can the individual or the community control that process. In our modern age of computers and high speed technology that question is probably more poignant that it was in Chardin's day. He many have thought, however, that the same poignancy applied to television, radios and air-traffic. As we become more complex our choices become more consequential. The study of ritual inhumanity can give us a view of both the benign and the malignant. Perhaps it can offer some guidance in how to decide in what direction we should pursue our further convolution and "Complexification."

The study of ritual inhumanity is tedious because of the repetition of the same events in diverse societies. It is frustrating because of the bias of observers. It is infuriating because of the lack of accurate information and detail. Yet it is the most fascinating of all subjects because the art is so typically human. There is a lesson in the study of ritual inhumanity that bears examination by the peoples of the world. If man and the world are to survive, the identity of the individual cannot be bypassed in favor of technology or economic expedience. We must all strive to recognize the right and the need of the individual to strive for identity and expression. His personal identity and its legitimate expressions are the truest forms of the <u>Tokens of Esteem</u>.

# About the Author

Pat Harvey was born in Wisconsin, grew up in the military and served six years in the Navy. He is a combat veteran of the Vietnam War. After his military service he attended college at Columbus State University where he earned a Bachelor's degree in History and a Master's degree in Education. He taught History and Political Science for some years at a small college in the South. This book is his first literary offering.

# *Notes*

La repetición de actitudes y fórmulas seculares no solamente asegura la permanencia del grupo en el tiempo, sino su unidad y cohesión. Los ritos y la presencia constante de los espiritus de los muertes entretejen un centro, un nudo de relaciónes que limitan la acción individual y protegan al hombre de la soledad y al grupo de la dispersión. (p.239)

The repetition of secular attitudes and formulas not only assured the permanence of the group in time but also its unity and cohesion. Rituals and the constant presence of spirits of the dead interjected a center, a nest of relations that limited individual action and protected man from solitude and the group from dispersion.

"Pour ce qui est de manger de la chair humaine, on peut dire qu'ils en faisant usage absolument comme nous de la viande de boucherie."

As to the eating of human flesh, one could say that they make use of it absolutely as we would of the meat from the butcher shop.

# Glossary

**Anthropophagy**
The act of cannibalism. Literally man eating.

**Arunta**
An ethnic group in central Australia composed of six separate tribal divisions.

**Ashanti**
The Ashanti lived in West Africa and were ruled by a divine king. They practiced a brutal dismemberment of their victims during the burial rite of the monarch.

**Ashurnarsipal**
Ashurnarsipal was an Assyrian king. When he conquered a nation he ordered his soldiers to cut off the hands and feet of the vanquished.

**Assurbanipal**
Assurbanipal was an Assyrian Monarch and conqueror of Babylon. He was noted for his extreme cruelty to the vanquished. He also built a great library at Nineveh.

**Aztecs**
Aztecs were native warrior people of Mexico who established hegemony over other native tribes shortly before the arrival of Spanish Explorers.

**Berserk**
Berserk was a special warrior among the Vikings known for fits of rage and violence.

## Callatiae
Callatiae were neighbors of the Greeks in ancient times. Herodotus reports that they ate the bodies of their deceased parents in order to preserve the parental spirits.

## Celts
A tribal people of ancient times. They were located throughout Western Europe and the British Isles. Most noted for their La Tene period of art.

## Churinga
Churinga was a sacred stone that each Arunta warrior received as a mark of his membership in the tribe.

## Circumcision
Circumcision was a common practice among many and diverse peoples. The prepuce of the male was removed in a coming of age ceremony.

## Cocam
Cocam was a tribal group of Meso-America. Warriors used the skulls of ancestors to make masks. These masks were worn on ceremonial occasions.

## Convivial Sacrifice
Convivial sacrifice is a ceremony in which the participants and the "gods" eat flesh. The participants and the gods were thought to share the feast.

## Crow Indians
Crow Indians were a people native to the Western Plains area of the United States. Their religion was centered upon dream and vision interpretation

## Cylinder Seal
A device, similar to a signet ring, with which ancient monarchs affixed their signature to documents.

## Devotio
Devotio was a sacrificial practice among the Roman Military nobles. Before the start of battle a Roman noble covered his head, charged into the opposing army and thereby sacrificed himself to the god of victory. The hope was that his sacrifice would insure victory.

## Diodorus Siculus
Siculus was a Greek historian that lived in the first century BC. He was noted for his description of the Celtic tribes

## Dolmen
A stone table or altar often used in sacrifice, especially human sacrifice.

## Druids
The Druids were Celtic priests that officiated at the sacrifice of war prisoners. In general they were the religious leaders among the Celts.

## Durga Puja
In Asssam, The Durga Puja was an autumn festival to the goddess Kali. A victim was beheaded and the head offered to the goddess

## Endocannibalism
Endocannibalism is a kind of cannibalism that occurs within a group. The primitive peoples believed that they could preserve the spirit and qualities of their own people by ingesting their remains.

## Excision
Excision or clitoridectomy was literally the circumcision of the female. This was a very painful and clearly useless procedure. The rite was associated with coming of age ceremonies.

### Exocannibalism
Exocannibalism is a kind of cannibalism that is directed outside one's own group. Primitives believed that they could add to the strength of their own tribe by ingesting the bodies of their enemies.

### Foramen Magnum
The large opening at the base of the skull through which the spinal cord is attached to the brain.

### Furor Teutonicus
This type of rage was attributed to the violence and audacity of the ancient Germanic tribes.

### Galla
The Galla was a tribe of Northern Africa. Among the Galla a young man was required to murder an enemy, usually in ambush, in order to advance in the tribal hierarchy.

### Genghis Khan
Genghis was a Mongol conqueror noted for decapitating conquered peoples. He had the heads arranged in piles so he could count the number of his victims.

### Great Mother Goddess
A deity worshipped throughout the Near East. She was considered to be the source of all life and sustenance.

### Great Sacrificial Stone
The stone based was used by Aztec priests to offer the hearts of their butchered victims to the Aztec gods.

### Holy Cave
The King of Zimbabwe was laid to rest in this burial chamber. Humans were butchered at the entrance to his grave during the funeral ceremonies.

## Homeopathic Magic

Homeopathic magic is the belief that one can exert power over another by possessing some part of the enemy. A voodoo doll is a good example.

## Incas

People native to Peru who developed a highly advanced civilization led by an emperor and a priestly hierarchy. Eventually conquered by the Spanish.

## Julius Caesar

Caesar was a Roman military commander in Gaul. He is famous for his account of the Gallic Wars.

## Jivaro

Natives of Ecuador known for their practice of shrinking heads. They remained largely isolated until modern times.

## Kalahari

The Kalahari desert is located in Southern Africa. The bushmen who dwell in the Kalahari amputated the little finger of the right hand of young men during the coming of age ceremony.

## Kali

In India, Kali was the Hindu goddess of death. Victims were offered to Kali in exchange for prosperity. Their heads were removed and used to make a necklace for the goddess.

## Kimbugwe

The Kimbugwe was an official among the Ganda. His sole function was to be the keeper of the king's umbilical cord. This cord was thought to have magical and sacred properties.

## Kiva

Among the Hopi Indians the Kiva was a ceremonial hut used for purification ceremonies.

### Kwakiutl Indians
Located in the Northwestern United States, the Kwakiutl were famous for their pot latches.

### Magi
The Magi were the priests of the ancient Persian religion. They practiced divination to determine future events.

### Manus
Manus were one of the native peoples of Melanesia. Their religion was based upon skull cults. Patrilineal social order.

### Marae
The Marae was a sacred burial site among the Tahitians. Most important rituals were performed on this sacred ground.

### Maya
The Maya were part of an advanced civilization in the Yucatan. Their culture was similar to that of the Incas and the Aztecs. Some ruins of their temple cities remain.

### Mbaya-guarca
Mbaya-guarca was a warrior tribe of central Brazil. They used the heads of their enemies as toys, drinking vessels and for other amusements.

### Melquart
Melquart was a Phoenician deity. The Phoenicians offered their children as sacrifices to Melquart, especially during times of stress or danger.

### Mochicha
The Mochicha was a small South American tribe contemporary with the Inca. Their method of sacrifice to the Jaguar god was defenestration.

## Neolithic

A word describing the New Stone Age, a period characterized by the rudimentary development of agriculture.

## Nero

Nero was the Roman emperor who tortured Christians by dipping them in tar and using them as torches in the halls of his palace.

## Nootka Indians

The Nootka were Amerindians of British Columbia. They were known for their practice of totally annihilating their enemies.

## Obsidian

A volcanic glass. When broken obsidian forms a razor sharp edge. Ancient peoples, notably the Aztecs, used obsidian to make knives and other cutting tools,

## Ocher

A rust colored mineral sometimes used in primitive rituals. Its reddish color was often used to depict blood in primitive art.

## Odin

Odin was the chief of the Nordic gods. Warriors feasted at Odin's table after a long day of fighting in Valhalla.

## Oracle Bones

Bones used by the Yin priests of the Shang Dynasty to divine the future.

## Paleolithic

A word describing the Old Stone Age, a period characterized by hunting, gathering societies.

## Pawnee Indians

The Pawnee were Amerindians from the Southwest. They sacrificed a corn maiden to the gods to insure a good harvest. Her body was cut into strips and buried in the fields.

### Pot latch
Among certain Indian tribes a pot latch was a contest between two rivals in which each tried to outdo the other by destroying as much of his personal property as possible.

### Romulus and Remus
Romulus and Remus were twins and the mythical founders of Rome. In a dispute one brother killed the other and became master of the city

### Royal Graves
These were tombs in Mesopotamia where the kings and queens of Ur were buried. Woolley excavated these sites and discovered lavish furnishings and human grave goods.

### Salamis
Salamis was the site of a naval battle in Ancient Greece between the Greeks and the Persians. The Greek commander, Themistocles, was victorious over the Persian king, Xerxes.

### Sand Hills
Sand Hills was the site of a massacre of Indians by the US Seventh Cavalry. The arms and the legs of the victims were cut off and later displayed as trophies. It is not to be confused with the more infamous Sand Creek Massacre.

### Scythians
Nomadic wagon people, circa eighth century before Christ. They were noted for their practice of suttee, particularly in the burial of their kings.

### Semang
The Semang were a people of Malaysia. They drew blood from them-

selves, mixed the blood with water and then threw the mixture into the rain. By doing this they hoped to appease Karei, the thunder god.

### Seutonius Paulinus
Paulinus was a Roman military commander in Britain in 61 AD. He engaged in a campaign to suppress the religious practices of the Druids.

### Shaman
In primitive tribes this was a witch doctor or Medicine man who was believed to possess great power. Shamans were thought to travel between the natural world and the spirit world.

### Shang
The first Chinese dynasty noted for the Yellow River Culture and highly prized bronze sculpture.

### Shipaya
Shipaya was a cannibal people of the Amazon. They killed their victims by shooting them with arrows. Then the warriors boiled the flesh of the victims for a feast

### Sinanthropus
Sinanthropus was an early hominid. His cave dwellings left remnants of hominid and animal bones mixed together. Some anthropologists suggest that he may have been a cannibal.

### Sumerians
The Sumerians were people who established one of the first major civilizations. Sumeria developed in the Tigris Euphrates river-valley. It was known for its temples and its cuneiform writing.

### Suttee
Literally it means true woman. When a man died in India his wife threw herself on his funeral pyre. More generically suttee refers to the practice of live burial and the use of human grave goods.

**Teutones**

An ancient Germanic tribe, the Teutones were noted for their use of hanging in sacrificing their victims to the god Odin.

**Thracians**

The Thracians were nomadic warriors that roamed in what is now Bulgaria. They were known for their hero cult worship and the use of human grave goods in their burials.

**Tinguians**

Tinguians were a tribe in Indonesia that practiced brain cannibalism.

**Topeth**

The Topeth was an outdoor altar made to function as an oven. Victims were passed through the fire of the oven as a sacrifice to the gods. This was a common practice among the Phoenicians.

**Trepanation**

Trepanation was a process of drilling a hole in the skull. Ancients believed that this would relieve pressure on the brain and act as a palliative or curative.

**Trobiand Islanders**

Trobiand culture was located among tribes in Melanesia. They buried the umbilical cord of a newborn in their yam garden. This was done to create a psychic link between the neonate and the family garden and to insure fertility.

**Tsantas**

Among the Jivaro a Tsantas was a fire-dried shrunken head. The head was thought to have religious and ceremonial properties.

**Tucuna**

Tucuna was a tribe of the Amazon. They believed that the life force of a person was located in his hair.

**Two Stage Burial**
Native peoples often buried the dead until the flesh rotted. The second stage was to unearth the remaining bones and place them in an ossuary.

**Valhalla**
This is the Viking notion of heaven. Warriors continued their day long fighting and night long drinking in Valhalla.

**Vedas**
Vedas lived in Ceylon. These warriors carried a piece of human liver in a pouch. When confronted with danger they chewed on the liver for strength and fortitude.

**Vegismal**
Vegismal refers to a period of twenty days. Some tribes used this time to purify themselves after they had killed and enemy.

**Vikings**
The Vikings were a seafaring Nordic group known for brutal assaults upon European cities. Viking literally means pirate.

**Voodoo**
Voodoo was part of a West African form of religion in which the body parts of a foe were used to cast a magic spell. Voodoo is a corruption of the African word Vodu.

**Wajoggo**
In East Africa, the Wajoggo threw an uncircumcised child into the river. This was a sacrifice in anticipation of a good harvest.

**Wanzo**
Among the Bambara of the Sudan, the Wanzo was an evil principle believed to exist in the prepuce or clitoris. The Bambara practiced excision and circumcision to expel this evil principle.

## War of the Flowers

During the reign of Montezuma the War of the Flowers was an athletic contest among the Aztecs. The winners sacrificed the losers to the gods.

## Witoto

Witoto clansmen were part of an indigenous people of Columbia and Peru. In their early stage of development they were also ritual cannibals.

## Yoga

Originally Yoga was a form of self-torture in India among the worshipers of Kali. Practitioners sought freedom from the desires of the flesh through strenuous exercise. They practiced methods of self-torture such as lying on beds of nails or walking on fiery coals.

## Ziggurat

A stepped pyramid used as a temple by the Babylonians. The most famous was the so-called Tower of Babel.

## Zulu

A sub-Saharan warrior people. Before European Colonization the Zulu tribes comprised a kingdom ruled by divine right monarchs.

# References

| | |
|---|---|
| Batey, Colleen | Cultural Atlas of the Viking World |
| Benedict, Ruth | Patterns of Culture |
| Bergamini, John | The Tragic Dynasty. A History of the Romanovs. |
| Breuil, Henri | The Men of the Old Stone Age. |
| Brown, Dee | Bury My Heart at Wounded Knee |
| Brownmiller, Susan | Against Our Will. Men, Women and Rape |
| Campbell, Joseph | The Masks of God |
| Caesar, Julius | The Gallic Wars |
| Chi, Li | The Beginnings of Chinese Civilization |
| Fol, Alexander | Thrace and the Thracians |
| France, Anatole | Les Dieux ont Soif |
| Frazier, James G. | The Golden Bough |
| Freud, Sigmund | Totem and Taboo |
| Galeano, Eduardo | Las Venas Abiertas de America Latina. |
| George, Katherine | "A Study in Ethnocentrism 1400-1800" in Montagu |
| Hays, H.R. | In the Beginnings |
| Herm, Gerhard | The Phoenicians. The Purple Empire |
| ——————— | The Celts. The People Who Came out of the Darkness |
| Herodotus | The Persian Wars |
| Jacobsen, Thorkild | The Treasures of Darkness |
| James, E.O. | The Origin of Sacrifice |
| Jones, Gwyn | A History of the Vikings |
| Levi-Strauss, Claude | Tristes Tropiques |

Livy, Titus                    The Early Hisltory of Rome

Lorenz, Konrad                 On Agression

Maijno, Guido                  The Healing Hand. Man and Wound

Malraux, Andre                 La Voie Royale

Maringer, Johannes             The Gods of Prehistoric Man

Money Kyrle                    The Meaning of Sacrifice

Montagu, Ashley ed.            The Comcept of the Primitive

Murdock, George                Our Primitive Contemporaries

Paz, Octavio                   El Laberinto de la Soledad

Plutarch                       The Rise and Fall of Athens

Russell, Jeffrey               The Devil. Perceptions of Evil

Shaw, Ian ed.                  The Oxford Encyclopedia of Ancient Egypt

Service, Elman                 A Profile of Primitive Culture

Teilhard de Chardin            Le Phenomene Humain

Tacitus                        The Annals of Imperial Rome

Tax, Sol                       "Primitive Man vs. Homo Sapiens" in Montagu

Vidal-Naquet, Pierre           Les Assassins de la Memoire

Woolley, Charles               Excavations at Ur

# Bibliography

Allen, J. Romilly.  Celtic Art: In Pagan and Christian Times. London: Bracken Books, 1993.

Andrews, Anthony. First Cities. Washington, D.C.: St. Remy Press and Smithsonian Institution, 1995

Baumann, Hans.  In the Land of Ur: The Discovery of Ancient Mesopotamia New York: Pantheon Books, 1969.

Benedict, Ruth.  Patterns of Culture. Houghton, Mifflin Company. Boston. 1934.

Benedict, Ruth.  Race: Science and Politics. 1940. Viking Press. New York. 1940.

Berdan, Frances.  Aztecs of Central Mexico: An Imperial Society. Holt, 1982.

Boas, Franz.   Race, Language, and Culture (1940)

———————   The Mind of Primitive Man (1911)

Brent, Peter.   The Viking Saga. New York: G.P. Putnam's Sons, 1975.

Breuil, Henri   The Men of the Old Stone Age. Greenwood Publishing. 1980.

Cambridge   The Cambridge History of Ancient China. Cambridge University Press, 1999.

Campbell, Joseph, The Power of Myth New York : Doubleday, c1988.

Campbell, Joseph, Historical Atlas of World Mythology. New York : Harper & Row, 1988.

Campbell, Joseph, Transformations of Myth Through Time New York : Perennial Library, c1990.

Campbell, Joseph, Myths, Dreams, and Religion Dallas, Tex.: Spring Publications, 1988, c1970.

Campbell, Joseph, The Masks of God New York : Arkana, 1991.

Carrasco, David  Daily Life of the Aztecs. People of the Sun and Earth. Westport: Greenwood Press, 1998.

Caso, Alfonso.          The Aztecs, People of the Sun. Norman: University of Oklahoma
                        Press, 1958.

Cernenko, E. N.         The Scythians, 700-300 B. C. Osprey Publishing, 1983

Chadwick, Nora.         The Celts. London: Penguin Books, 1971.

Crawford, Harriet.      Sumer and the Sumerians. New York: Cambridge University
                        Press, 1991.

Delaney, Frank.         The Celts. Glasgow: Harper Collins, 1986.

Ellis, Peter.           The Celtic Empire: The First Millenium of Celtic History 1000 BC–
                        51 AD. London: Constable and Company, Ltd., 1990.

Eluère, Christiane.     The Celts: Conquerors of Ancient Europe. New York: Harry N.
                        Abrams, Inc., 1993

Farrel, R. T., ed.      The Vikings. London: Philllimore, 1982.

Fitzhugh, W.            Vikings : The North Atlantic Saga. Washington, DC : Smithsonian
                        Institution Press in association with the National Museum of Natu-
                        ral History, c2000.

Fol, Alexander          Thrace and the Thracians. Saint Martin's Press, 1977

Frankfort, Henri A      The Intellectual Adventure of Ancient Man. University of Chicago
                        Press, 1977

Frazer, James G.        The Golden Bough. A Study in Magic and Religion. Penguin
                        books, 1996.

France, Anatole         Les Dieux Ont Soif. Classic Books, {1844, 1924, 2001}

Fuentes, Carlos.        El Espejo Enterrado. Mexico: Fondo de Cultura Economica, 1992.

Galeano, Eduardo        Las Venas Abiertas de America Latina. Distribooks Intl., 1994.

Herm, Gerhard.          The Celts: The People Who Came Out of Darkness. New York:
                        Barnes & Noble Books, 1993.

Herm, Gerhard           The Phoenicians. The Purple Empire of the Ancient World. William
                        Morrow Co., 1975.

Hildinger, Erik         Warriors of the Steppe. Perseus Books Group, 1997.

Jacobsen, Thorkild      The Treasures of Darkness. The History of Mesopotamian Reli-
                        gion. Yale University Press, l986.

James, E.O.             The Origin of Sacrifice. A Study in Comparative Religion. Kennkat
                        Press.

James, Simon.          The World of the Celts. London: Thames and Hudson, Ltd.,1993.

Jones, Gwyn            A History of the Vikings. New York : Oxford University Press, 1985.

Kramer, Samuel         History Begins at Sumer: Thirty-Nine Firsts in Man's Recorded
                       History. Philadelphia: University of Pennsylvania Press, 1981.

Kramer, Samuel         The Sumerians: Their History, Culture, and Character. Chicago:
                       University of Chicago Press, 1963.

Leon-Portilla, M. ed.  The Broken Spears: An Aztec Account of the Conquest of Mexico.
                       Beacon, 1962

Levi-Strauss, C.       Tristes Tropiques New York: MacMillan, 1974.

Magnusson, M.          Vikings New York : Dutton, 1980.

Majno, Guido,          The Healing Hand: Man and Wound in the Ancient World Cam-
                       bridge, MA: Harvard University Press, 1975.

Malpass, Michael.      Daily Life in the Inca Empire. Westport: Greenwood Press, 1996.

Mead, Margaret.        Blackberry Winter: My Earlier Years. New York: William Morrow &
                       Company, Inc., 1972.

_____             Coming of Age in Saomoa, 1928.

Montagu, Ashley.       Man's Most Dangerous Myth: Fallacy of Race. Altamira Press,
                       1997.

Montagu, Ashley ed.    The Concept of Race. New York: MacmMillan, 1969.

Paz, Octavio           El Laberinto de la Soledad y Otras Obras. Penguin Putnam, 1997

Poertner, Rudolf.      The Vikings :Rise and Fall of the Norse Sea Kings. New York : St.
                       Martin's Press, c1975.

Powell, T.G.           The Celts. London: Thames and Hudson, Ltd., 1958.

Roesdahl, Else.        The Vikings New York : Penguin Books, 1992, c1987.

Russell, Jeffrey.      The Devil. Perception of Evil From Antiquity to Primitive Christian-
                       ity. New York:Cornell University Press, 1977.

Sawyer, P. H.          Kings and Vikings: Scandinavia and Europe. AD 700-1100. Lon-
                       don: Routledge, 1982.

_____             The Oxford Illustrated History of the Vikings. New York : Oxford
                       University Press, c1997.

Service, Elman R.    Cultural Evolutionism: Theory in Practice. New York: Holt, Rine-
                     hart, and Winston, 1971.

Service, Elman R.    Profiles in Ethnology Addison-Wesley Publishing, 1997.

Service, Elman R.    A Profile in Primitive Culture.

Sharer, Robert.      Daily Life in Maya Civilization. Westport: Greenwood Press, 1996.

Simpson, J.          The Viking World. New York: St. Martin's Press, 1980.

Simpson, Judith      Ancient China. Time-Life, 1999

Tacitus, Cornelius.  The Histories. Clarendon Press, 1912

_____          The Annals of Imperial Rome.

Teilhard de Chardin  The Phenomenon of Man. New York: Harper and Row, 1975

Vidal-Naquet, P.     Les Assassins de la Mémoire. "Un Eichmann de Papier" et Autres
                     Essais sur le Révisionnisme. Paris: La Découverte, 1987.

Weaver, Muriel.      The Aztecs, Maya, and Their Predecessors Archeology of
                     Mesoamerica. New York: Seminar Press, 1972.

Wenke, Robert.       Patterns in Prehistory. New York: Oxford University Press, 1990.

Wilson, David.       The Vikings and Their Origins; Scandinavia in the First Millennium.
                     New York: McGraw-Hill [c1970]

Winstone, H.V.       Woolley of Ur: The Life of Sir Leonard Woolley. London: Secker
                     and Warburg, 1990.

Woolley, C.          The Sumerians. New York: W. W. Norton, 1965.

_____          Ur of the Chaldees Ithaca, New York: Cornell University Press,
                     1982.

_____          Discovering the Royal Tombs at Ur. New York: Macmillan, 1969.

Woolley, C.          Excavations at Ur: A Record of Twelve Years Work. New York:
                     Crowell, 1955.

0-595-22288-9

www.ingramcontent.com/pod-product-compliance
Lightning Source LLC
Chambersburg PA
CBHW061356280526
45784CB00001B/281